Addicted to Love

CLARE
CATFORD

Addicted to Love

From Rehab to Heaven?

DARTON · LONGMAN + TODD

First published in 2008 by
Darton, Longman and Todd Ltd
1 Spencer Court
140–142 Wandsworth High Street
London SW18 4JJ

ISBN–10: 0–232–52728–8
ISBN–13: 978–0–232–52728–5

A catalogue record for this book is available from
the British Library.

Designed and produced by Sandie Boccacci
Set in 11/12.75pt Apollo
Printed and bound in Great Britain by
Cromwell Press, Trowbridge, Wiltshire

CONTENTS

This book is dedicated to all those
who are broken,
who struggle and
who want to find freedom,
peace of mind and
God in that place.

Introduction

$\mathcal{M}$y name's Clare and I'm a recovering addict. If you know what it's like to be unable to stop drinking, taking drugs, eating, working, shopping or obsessing over a relationship, the idea of addiction will need no explanation. If you feel you are in control of your life, bear with me; we may have more in common than you realise.

According to recent statistics, addiction is commonplace. Possibly 75 million lives in the USA are seriously affected by alcoholism, some 60 per cent of women and 50 per cent of men have eating disorders, and it is estimated that many thousands suffer from work addiction or sexual addiction.[1]

Friends and family would often comment on my eating habits. 'What diet are you on now?' my parents would ask. 'Why can't you come down the pub with us? It'll be a laugh!' friends would say, not realising that I had spent the day bingeing and purging and felt too exhausted to go out, terrified of the pub chips that might be on the menu.

There are many theories as to why one person is an addict and another is not. Experts have debated whether some of us have a genetic disposition to addictive behaviour; others claim environmental factors are more influential.

The explanation that makes most sense to me is the counsellor and theologian John Bradshaw's theory. His

1

conclusions are drawn from observations formed after working with addicts for many years. He believes that:

> the drivenness in any addiction is about the rup-tured self, the belief that one is flawed as a person. The content of the addiction, whether it is alcoholism or work, is an attempt at an intimate relationship. The workaholic with her work, or the alcoholic with his booze, are having a love affair. Each one mood alters to avoid the feeling of loneliness and hurt in the underbelly of shame.[2]

The common strand is the addict's powerlessness over their behaviour; we cannot just 'stop' drinking, taking drugs or eating compulsively.

Food was where my powerlessness first emerged. Unable to express my emotions and lacking in confidence, I ate to blot out the pain. In my early twenties I was the leader of and an actor in Footprints, a theatre company that performed plays with Christian themes in primary and secondary schools throughout the UK. On the surface I was confident and capable. Underneath I was hurting badly. On one trip to a school in Glasgow, I wandered around the shopping centre, bingeing on chocolate and cakes and topping it off with gallons of diet coke. I then threw the whole lot up in the public loos as quietly and as secretly as I could. Staring down the toilet was a familiar activity for me – degrading, and debilitating.

'Are you all right?' came a voice from the loo attendant on one occasion. 'Fine, just fine,' I cheerfully answered back, 'just a bit of a stomach ache, I'll be out in a minute.' I would then pray that she had no idea what I was doing, and leave the loo giving her a cheery smile and wave, pretending to fix my make-up.

Eating disorders are complex and deep-rooted, and cause great suffering. They occur as a result of childhood trauma, huge personal insecurity and as a way of dealing with feelings that seem overwhelming and unbearable. I was bulimic for fifteen years; it began in my late teens and ended in my early thirties. I would binge uncontrollably in order to fill a gnawing inner emptiness, and then throw up, trying to purge the anger and fear from my system.

Although my eating disorder contributed to the end of my marriage, I do not believe it was the main cause. I had no idea who I was, what I wanted or where I was going. Staying in the marriage – even though we both worked at it in Relate for over a year – was just not an option for me. I needed to be alone, to heal emotional wounds that were still unresolved from childhood. I could not see another way.

Having moved out of the marital home, I can remember sitting in my rented flat surrounded by packing boxes crying over a Christmas fairy that I had found amongst the wreckage. My thoughts ran riot, and I alternated between terror and sick-making anxiety. 'Who is going to look after me now?' I said to myself over and over again. 'Who is going to hold me, care for me and listen to me?'

My shame ran so deep and the terror of being alone was so overwhelming that I could not bear to be on my own. Sadly, with the end of my marriage went my friends too. No one from the church we went to contacted me, and I had been so focused on my career that I had not built up a support network of close and caring girl-friends. I was out of work, so I had no colleagues around me either. There was one person, apart from my parents, who I spoke to regularly and who stood by me during this time. I would ring her weeping and ask, 'When will I feel better? When will the pain end?' She listened lovingly and gave me what support she could. I will never forget how she cared for me, and we are still friends now.

At the time I blamed everyone for this situation, including myself. 'Why did no one phone me from the church? How can they call themselves Christians? And where's God when I need him?' I would wail in my small rented living room. The truth, as I later discovered, was that no one knew how to get in touch, and were not sure whether or not I wanted them to. In that isolated and dark place I felt abandoned, like that small child from an old NSPCC advert, sitting head bowed, socks by her ankles on the end of an unmade bed, dejected and alone.

Over the weeks I became obsessed with the thought that perhaps another relationship would make the pain go away. And I went out to find one, fuelled by women's magazine articles that suggested dating after divorce was healthy and normal.

I met my first new boyfriend training for the London marathon. He was kind, and fun to be with and for a while this nagging emptiness temporarily eased. But I began to become increasingly unhappy as I lost myself. I had not healed after the divorce, or resolved some of the bigger, deeper issues from my childhood. Eventually I began to feel more and more trapped and uncomfortable to the point that I had to pull away. This led to such terrible feelings of abandonment and withdrawal that I could only ease the situation by resuming the existing relationship or by beginning a new one; it was a destructive and desperate pattern. I began to realise that I did not know who I was, how God fitted into this confusion, and how on earth I was going to heal.

Relationship or sex and/or love addiction is very hard to admit to, particularly in a Christian context. It conjures up images of promiscuity on a grand scale, endless one-night stands and fleeting liaisons. This not my experience but even if it was, I believe a helpful response isn't to shame the addict but to support them as they begin to discover their powerlessness over the compulsion to use relationships to alter their mood. A love addict can have had endless partners or none at all, spending their time living from the fantasies in their head, which can be just as compelling. The idea of 'co-dependence' is far more acceptable – the tendency to stay in and return to relationships that may not be appropriate for us, because we fear abandonment and loneliness, and the belief that another human being will take responsibility for us and look after us, because we cannot look after ourselves. The result, however you define it, is the same. We become isolated from friends, ourselves and from God. The common thread is the belief that someone else will take the pain away.

When my marriage ended, I sincerely believed that if I threw myself into another, different partnership, I would be complete. This is 'textbook' love addict behaviour; the idea that someone else will 'make me all right' because deep down I didn't believe that I was 'enough' or ever would be.

It is only now, after serial attempts at supposed intimacy, culminating in a relationship with a married man (whose marriage I was not aware of); and then a near-miss affair with a married Christian man that was far more in my head than in my bed, that I have begun to look at this part of my personality. I am learning that God wants to heal my deepest wounds, and that by trusting this power greater than myself I can be restored to sanity. This is an ongoing journey, which I would never have embarked upon without support from other recovering addicts, and without the help of a wise therapist and other key mentors along the way. The emptiness I felt, and sometimes still feel, has prompted me to explore my relationship with God at a profound level, and although I cannot say I am healed, and I still feel so vulnerable at times, I can say that my life is improving beyond my wildest dreams.

*

You can't stop it. You keep eating, furtively nipping to the garage or corner shop to stock up on chocolate and cake, digging your fingers into the icing and stuffing your face most of the way back home.

You keep a bottle of 'something' in the house, just to give you a little pick up when the kids get out of control, you have a row with your spouse, or your parents get difficult on the phone. Soon you are knocking back nips of vodka or wine at ten in the morning, and brushing your teeth so that no one will smell it on your breath when you pick up the kids on the school run.

You have to have just one more pair of shoes. Your stomach tenses with excitement as you touch the smooth leather, and you slump into despair after the purchase, realising that there's not enough cash in your bank account. You throw the shoes, still in their box, into the back of the wardrobe, where they rest alongside all the other unworn clothes still with their labels intact.

You cannot bear to let your boyfriend go. You keep texting and emailing him, convinced that the two of you are destined to be together, even though he has said 'no' a million times.

You cannot go to bed before checking your work emails one more time, or your mobile in case a client has called. You get a buzz from feeling that you can work all hours, even if that means your relationship suffers and you never see the kids.

You attend every church meeting going, sign up for every Christian conference, read your Bible whenever you can, and pray around the clock, in the belief that you are getting closer to God and that he smiles on such fervent commitment.

You love your wife, but are compelled to seek sex with strangers, pore over porn magazines, visit sex sites on the net and watch adult videos over and over again. 'It's just what red-blooded healthy men do, isn't it?' But deep down you have an uneasy feeling that something might be wrong.

Whether it's drugs, shopping, food, alcohol, people or even religion, if the habit becomes unmanageable, you are an addict. I suspect addiction is far more common amongst Christians than many of us would admit, and in particular sex and love addiction. There is often so much fear associated with being honest and open about sexual desire and relationships in these circles, that the feelings are driven underground where they become even more potent. Most of us know what we 'should' do, but when the compulsion takes over, 'shoulds', 'oughts' and 'musts' carry no weight, particularly if our shame is deeply felt. I have often heard sermons or talks that humiliate those who use pornography. My own response is one of compassion – does the speaker have any idea what it must feel like to be unable to put it down? Of course we have to take responsibility for our actions, but sometimes the compulsion to behave in ways that we know are damaging to others and to ourselves is so great that it is hard to see a way out. I have found that by humbly admitting my powerlessness over my behaviour, I been able to begin to do something about it. This is not an overnight solution, though. And I hope this book will go some way to explain how freedom from addictive behaviour can be achieved.

This book is also written for those who need compassion, not judgement. I am not in any way using relationship addiction as an excuse to indulge in rampant sexual or immoral behaviour, exciting though it may sound. As an adult I *want* to take responsibility for my life. Recognising powerlessness, and allowing God into that pain is, I believe, a way of achieving that end. I am still a 'work-in-progress' and my own dark night of the soul is not over, but increasingly I feel more at ease in my own company and the compulsion to pursue yet another relationship is subsiding. I have never experienced a quick divine fix. My journey has been one of painful self-discovery, and a very gradual awakening to the fact that there really is an all-powerful and loving God who wants to help me arrest my addictive disease.

So why does addiction start and where does it come from in the first place? And how is it arrested? And in the depths of my despair, what happened when I ended up on the kitchen floor, pills at my side, ready to take my own life? This is my story.

ONE

Hospital Blues

$\mathcal{M}$y legs throbbed. I cried out, 'I want my mum. Where is Mum?' A starched nurse appeared and gave me some painkillers. I slipped into a black hole of nothingness. I was six years old. When I woke up, my mother and sister were sitting by my metal hospital bed. I could see my mother anxiously twisting her hands, saying, 'Are you all right? Mum's here,' and I cried louder and asked for my favourite toy, a little furry monkey that I would not let out of my sight.

Despite their love and care I felt very alone, depressed and frightened, trapped in plaster from my waist to my toes. Incarcerated in that plaster I felt imprisoned and powerless. Little did I know then how significant that experience would be. All through my adult life I have been afraid of that feeling of claustrophobia; and I have always panicked when it is triggered, either by people or circumstances.

The reason for the operation was my legs. I did not walk early, and was taken to a specialist to find out why. He discovered that my hips were slightly twisted and I needed an operation to correct the problem. He was a kind and gentle man. 'Now Clare,' he would urge, 'walk up and down this corridor for me, that's a good girl.' Always anxious to please, I trotted up and down the imposing hospital corridor as tall and proud as I could so that I wouldn't have to go into hospital, the voice in my head saying, 'Try hard, walk straight, you can do it!' But he decided to operate and I tried to hold back the tears when mum and dad told me the news.

To a child, any hospital in the 1960s would have been imposing. The green NHS paint on all the walls and the smell of strong disinfectant in the wards was enough to rattle even the heartiest adult. All the nurses had that cheery tone which is meant to make you feel at ease. 'Pop up here, Clare', 'Just a small pin prick, it won't hurt', 'Deep breaths', and so on. But underneath I was very scared, no matter how upbeat the staff.

The day of the operation came and I felt groggy and tired as the anaesthetic took effect. No matter how often the nurses tried to reassure me – 'Don't worry, you will be all right. You'll wake up soon, and it will all be over' – I wasn't convinced. I was anxious and nervous. I went to sleep being able to move my little legs and woke up in great pain, immobilised in plaster from my waist to my feet. My mother visited the hospital every day; it was a 25-mile round trip. My sister was a toddler, so these visits must have been exhausting and draining for them both. Mum made a special scrapbook with get-well cards from all my friends, and some of them came to visit. One particular family gave me plastic flies (who knows why!) and I lost them all down the plaster and had to get them out with a knitting needle, avoiding my stitches. Well, it passed the time. Nowadays, hospitals provide psychologists to support parents and help children through such stressful times. This service was not available in the 1960s and the terror and loneliness I felt every time my mother left were terrible.

My parents made every effort to make sure that I had the support I needed from them at this time. Having a sick child is possibly one of the toughest challenges any parent can face. But despite that effort, being left alone in my hospital bed for what felt like an eternity, with no professional I could turn to, left me in a bad way. Children's wards now, compared to children's wards then, are so, so different. Today they have colour on the walls, pictures everywhere, child psychologists available, and parents are given the choice to stay overnight if they wish. Then there were grey municipal walls, nurses who didn't seem to be attached to the children's ward per se, and little or no schooling.

I am not describing an Oliver Twist-style workhouse, where doctors towered over neglected children who were lucky to be wearing hospital issue rags, but the hospital was not child-focused or really child-centred. I know that plenty of children went through and continue to go through this kind of trauma. But even to this day, and this has been backed up by the professionals whose help I have sought as an adult, that experience left me not only physically but mentally scarred. The physical scars I still find intriguing – they are like zips on each side of my leg, and have never really worried me. They are a source of great fascination and fun for small children who have broken their own legs or arms! Of more concern was the depression that first seemed to emerge inside at this young age, and that has really plagued me ever since.

There were a couple of people I encountered on the ward who made a difference. My consultant had a lovely manner and even when he was describing how he was going to cut my thighs open, twist the bones like Playdoh, and put in metal pins to hold it all together, he made it sound like a walk in the park! There was also a great physiotherapist. I was sent home briefly, in plaster, as it was important to give my bones enough time to heal. I loved being in a cherishing environment again and my parents had rigged up a special bedroom for me to use, complete with internal phone and bedpan! Once my plaster had been removed, I had to return to the hospital, which is when I first encountered the kind physiotherapist. I discovered I had thick black downy hair covering my skin from my hips to my feet, since my legs hadn't seen natural light for a number of months. The physiotherapist's job was to get me to walk again, first by strengthening my legs in a pool, and then helping me to stand upright on solid ground.

She never laughed at my funny, duck-like legs, but held me gently and encouraged me to bend my knees, as small droplets of blood leaked into the water from the stitches that had yet to come out. That pool was warm and welcoming and I was always asking if I could go for more sessions. Despite these happier moments, my overwhelming memory of this time is a black depression that would often overwhelm me when my mother left to go home with my sister after visiting time, and the mood would stay firmly entrenched until they came back either the next day or later in the week.

I felt overwhelmed in that hospital bed – trapped and angry. There is a parallel with my life today, as I have felt overwhelmed in other areas of my life, too. Men, my parents, and jobs; I have allowed these things in their way to overpower me, thinking that 'they' must be right and 'I' must be wrong, and I had better toe the line or I would be left out in the cold. The thought of being 'overwhelmed by God and his Spirit' terrifies me to such an extent that I have always been frightened of having a dramatic overpowering experience of God, too.

I have learned over the years that God's Spirit is not going to be invasive or abusive. What matters is not how I appear to other people, in church or out, but who I am in all my complexity, sadness and joy.

In hospital most of the nurses and doctors were kind, but there was one who seemed to take an instant dislike to me and resent the fact that I had so much parental attention. I was a child of middle-class parents, who could afford to buy me toys and games. The little frail girl with a spinal injury in the bed opposite had nothing by comparison. Her parents rarely visited and this particular nurse lavished attention on her, for understandable reasons, except that they weren't understandable to me as a child. With me, she was rough and unkind, and I didn't want her near me. She told me to 'Buck up and stop complaining.' 'No tears now, be a good girl', she scolded. 'Please sit up', she commanded. 'Don't make a fuss, it doesn't hurt that much!' – when it did. I refused to go the loo as a kind of protest; it was the one thing I felt I had control over. She gave me an enema, which another nurse said wasn't necessary, and I sat on the bedpan, feeling humiliated, angry and degraded.

I remember falling into that black hole in my head, panicking because I felt so trapped in the plaster, and vowing that once the plaster came off I would never get myself in a position where I would have to trust a grown-up so completely again. I believe this was my first real experience of depression but, as a child, I had no way of knowing that or processing it. It felt like being trapped in a huge metal cage from which there was no escape. I also remember praying to God, who for some reason I had complete faith in, to help me and keep me safe. 'God', I said, 'I am scared and lonely and I want some friends, can you help me?' I've no idea whether the prayer was answered, but that day the consultant came round and was kind to me, so perhaps it was. Either way, it was the start of a life-long dialogue that still goes on, despite my many ups and downs. There was no particular religious tradition in my family, but in my vulnerability I continued talking to him in my head, chattering incessantly when I was particularly frightened.

When the day arrived for me to go home, I felt fear and relief in equal measure. I travelled home in an ambulance as I was still in plaster, my legs fixed in a scissor shape. The nurses lifted me from the back of the van into the converted room that my parents had prepared for me, complete with that internal phone so that I could ring their bedroom from my new bed.

I was thrilled to see my father, too. He was often away working, as he was an airline pilot. I have always craved my father's attention – longed and searched for it – and when he gave it, in his way, I did not recognise it. The circumstances were not ideal, but I had his attention at last. By a strange twist of fate, my father had been travelling as a passenger on a plane that caught fire on take-off. He damaged his leg helping others to escape, and both of us were now in plaster, recovering. I remember how thrilled I was when he lifted me, still in my plaster cast, and whirled me around the room even though his own leg was broken, and I felt safe – the focus of his attention and of his love.

As I progressed into my teens, a rather gawky and awkward girl, I began to focus on my weight, worrying about the size of my jeans and the shape of my stomach. My mother and her friends seemed to be permanently on a diet, and my school friends were always cutting out chocolate and cake to get 'thin' for the dire discos that were the highlight of the weekend. For many this would have been a mere teenage phase to grow out of and move on from. For me, though, it was different. I wasn't overweight to start with, but I made a mental association between control and the amount I ate. Frightened of what I thought were unacceptable feelings, such as anger, rage or frustration, I focused all my attention on calorie counting and fat units. The payoff? In the first place I stopped having to feel. I began to starve and then binge, eating the entire contents of the larder and then trying to hide the empty packets and wrappings under my bed. Eventually, it became a never-ending

14

cycle that I simply could not break. I would stand on the bathroom scales with one foot, willing them to show a weight loss, but that never happened. I gained about ten pounds and loathed myself for my lack of self-control. This simply made the problem worse and I would vow to diet again 'tomorrow'.

Against this backdrop, I was very curious about God. As a younger child I had had an unwavering faith, which I cannot really explain, and this became a sceptical hunger as I got older. Choruses and prayers at the school Christian Union meetings infuriated me – I thought everyone was so 'wet'! I frequently disrupted those gatherings, partly for attention, but partly to find answers to the whys and wherefores of human existence. Curiously, I was more interested in theological questions than many of my contemporaries who seemed happy enough gossiping about which eyeshadow to wear at the weekend and how much jewellery they could get away with alongside the school uniform. Perhaps if I'd been better adjusted I would have followed their example, but when I wasn't bingeing or starving I felt empty, desperately spiritually empty, and I wanted to find an answer to that soulful yearning.

I had a genuine conversion experience in my teens, at a CYFA camp – a teenage holiday that focused on the Christian life. I'd picked up a leaflet discarded on the school floor, and I went home announcing to my mother my intention to go on the holiday. She rang the vicar who'd organised the holiday to check 'it wasn't the Moonies', and off I went with the required Bible in my luggage, although mine was an out-of-date version my parents had managed to rustle up from the darkest recesses of the bookshelves.

'The House Party Welcomes You!' That phrase, highlighted in bright letters above the entrance, greeted me when I arrived on the coach from the station. I was confused. If this was a party where was the drink, and where was the disco? No one was dancing, and no one was drinking. 'How odd,' I thought. 'Who are these people?' A hippie with long hair, flat sandals and a cheesecloth shirt greeted me at the door. I wanted to get back on that coach. 'These people are just weird,' I thought.

People kept asking me the same question, in cheery upbeat voices. 'Have you been on a house party before?' 'No,' I said, rather defensively. And I thought, 'And I never want to come again'. It was a complete culture shock: prayer meetings where teenagers fervently talked aloud with their eyes closed, big knees-ups at night where the hippie with the long hair played the guitar and asked us to join in with songs that I'd never heard of but that everyone else knew by heart.

I spoke to my 'dorm leader' – the term seems rather quaint now. 'I can't stand this,' I said. 'I feel like I'm being brainwashed!' She told me to 'hang in there,' but most of the time I preferred to hang out with the harder-looking girls who kept nipping out for a smoke.

The kindness got to me in the end, though. Even though I had, at first, thought the people over-nice and rather sickly, with no fashion sense, they genuinely seemed to care, and they affirmed me in ways I hadn't been used to. I developed immediate crushes on some of the more attractive male leaders, and I would loiter round the swimming pool trying to look sexy in my Marks and Sparks bikini. I was too shy to flirt with the boys, even though I thought about it, so I focused on the 'talks' instead. They were rather formulaic, building up to 'The Way' talk at the end of the week, explaining how Jesus died for our sins and set us free.

'Good for him,' I thought. 'But he needn't have bothered. I didn't ask him to make all that effort.' I have come to understand that the reason I felt that way was that, as a shame-based human, my greatest sin was not to value myself enough. I cannot believe that God thinks I am a worm who should be grateful for what he did for me. That reinforces my guilt and pain; it does not set me free from it. Of course a more mature understanding of Jesus' life and actions has helped me to see that I am valued more than I can ever imagine, but I still struggle to believe that.

There were other, lifestyle-type talks, too. Two rather overweight leaders, who were married to each other, spoke about how they had lost their virginity on their wedding night. I don't mean to be cruel, but the thought of either of them having sex was a little off-putting, to say the least. I noticed a great emphasis on abstaining from sex before marriage that, considering I hadn't even got a boyfriend, seemed premature. Still, despite the embarrassment, their talk raised some intriguing questions about relationships.

The end of the week arrived and on the last night I felt an overwhelming desire to ask God into my life. I don't know why, and I fought the urge tooth and nail, but I prayed the 'prayer' and felt a sense of peace and connection that I hadn't felt before. I felt a reassurance that I was OK, and my very active brain was soothed by whatever happened. I supposed, once I got home, that I had 'become a Christian', though I had no real idea what that meant.

My parents were understandably cautious about my new-found faith. One Sunday lunch, in between roast lamb and ice cream, I announced with great passion, 'You know you will go to hell if you don't become a Christian!' My father told me to 'Stop being daft,' and my mother said, 'You've been brainwashed by that holiday; I wish you'd never been.' I went to my room in tears, lamenting, as teenagers do, that 'no one understands me'. Their reactions were completely understandable, but I used those responses as proof of how different 'from them' I was becoming, and my new Christian identity gave me something to cling onto when I felt depressed or lonely. Genuine though this conversion was, it was also, in part, a teenage rebellion against what I considered to be a family environment lacking in any real show of emotion. Christianity gave me a language to express things I hadn't been able to before. But, as I tried to be a 'perfect disciple', I also found that my sense of shame and self-loathing increased, as I failed in my attempts to stop compulsively overeating.

My view of God, at that time, was very restricted, and also inaccurate. I had always been told that God was loving and just, but deep down, if I am honest, I had difficulty believing the truth of that statement. Priests and older Christians would say, 'Clare, God loves you as you are.' But I could not believe them. How could God love a bulimic? Surely I did not deserve love, but punishment?

TWO

Family Matters

$\mathcal{M}$y experience of love and what it means was not really clear in my childhood although my parents, as most parents do, did the best they could and I have no doubt now that they loved me and continue to do so. As a small child I was nervous, creative and sensitive. My own father, although loving in his own way, was largely absent throughout my childhood because of his work as a pilot, so I had no firm reference point when it came to understanding what fatherhood really meant. In order to please my parents, I unconsciously tried to read their minds, and become what I thought they wanted me to be in order to gain their approval and love. This meant that I learned to keep quiet if I thought an opinion, a belief or a behaviour would upset them, and I shut down the bits of my personality that I felt were not acceptable. I tried so hard to be a 'good girl'. The great psychoanalyst, Carl Jung, calls this creating a false self. At school, however, I let my personality run riot. When I was 11 my mother was approached at a parents' evening by one of the teachers who asked, 'Is Clare as difficult and disruptive at home as she is in the class-room? She won't concentrate and spends her time trying to distract the others.' My mum came home, horrified. 'I didn't recognise you from what the teacher said. You sounded like a different child!' I was.

To some extent we all do this. At work, in church, or

in our relationships, we don't show the parts of our personality that are angry or full of rage in case we are rejected by others and, if we have a faith, by God. Of course those bits are as much a part of me as the bits I want you to see, and those bits are accepted by God too since God sees all of us in our entirety. The Bible is full of dysfunctional men and women whom God uses to do his work. Abraham, Moses and David, to name three, are all powerfully flawed and human; real flesh and blood human beings who step out of line, encounter God's unwavering love, and step out of line again.

Our own culture does not help either. In one of his many books, the Catholic priest Henri Nouwen writes:

> In our competitive world we are so used to thinking in terms of 'more' or 'less', that we cannot easily see how God can love all human beings with the same unlimited love while at the same time loving each of them in a totally unique way. Somehow, we think we can only fully enjoy our being loved by God if others are loved less than we are.[1]

My mother was very loving in many ways when I was growing up but also, if I am honest, capable of great rages, and she had the ability to terrify me. I can see now that this stemmed from some of her own childhood frustration and pain. Her younger years were hard and lonely, and my parents' 'get on with it' generation were not encouraged to look at their own past emotional wounds – this would have been regarded as too self-indulgent. She was an evacuee in the Channel Islands during the German occupation, and although her own mother loved her, she did not appear to be able to show it. I hazard a guess that my mother felt abandoned in those young years, and those wounds, if they are not processed, do tend to stay with us.

We had no real Christian tradition in our family,

although my parents are moral and caring people. I had that experience of God in my teens, on the CYFA holiday, and although I heard people say that God's love was not finite, I could not believe that there was enough to go round as I had always felt that in order to gain my parents' love I had to try harder and be better behaved. I approached relationships in the same way. I remember as a teenager being delirious with joy after being asked out at one of those hideous 1970s discos where boys were at one end of the room and girls were at the other. 'You want ta dance?' asked the blond 'hunk' (such a 1970s word!) who I had fancied for weeks. And we glued ourselves together as 10 CC's 'I'm Not in Love' boomed out of the stereo and girls and boys stuck like leeches to each other, thinking that this was the way to be fully-fledged grown-ups. We split up a week later, but I can still recall the overwhelming feeling and rush of adrenalin I felt when he showed an interest in me, despite my flares, curly perm and Marks and Spencer chain-mail belt! (This was before the Twiggy ads.) Subsequently I felt that if a man showed me affection then I had better grab it quick before it disappeared, whether or not it was right for me, or the man involved.

Alongside experimenting with blue eyeshadow from Woolworths and smudging my first mascara, I lay on my bedroom floor, with a coat-hanger in my jeans' zip, trying to get into the smallest size possible. I obsessed about calories, then ate all my friends' school lunches and tried to starve at home in the evening. We had endless fights about this at home. 'If you don't eat, you will raid the biscuit tin when my back is turned,' my mum would say. I would try and convince her that I was not hungry: 'I had a huge lunch, I don't need any more!' And when she wasn't looking I would grab cakes out of the larder when, inevitably, I felt starving later on. The

21

bathroom scales seemed to have a voice of their own. 'Aha! You are heavier ... again! Starve yourself girl, drink less, and you will be thinner and perfect!'

A child's attachment to his or her parents is a complex business. Through feeding as a child, the small baby and then the toddler learns trust; as the early years go by the child tests out its independence but with constant reference to its parents, finding security in their presence. If something upsets or gets in the way of this process then the ensuing trauma can, say some health professionals, have a great impact on the pleasure areas of the brain. In other words, trauma can, some mental health professionals believe, almost rewire a child's brain so that the 'feel good' chemicals, like serotonin, are not produced in the amounts that they should be. This, in turn, means that the child will have a tendency to depression in later life; and if one or other parent has suffered, the chances of getting ill are even greater. This explanation should not be taken as scientific fact, although it is based upon well-established psychological theory.

However, having sought psychiatric help in recent years for depression, and examined the reasons that may lie behind it, this theory makes logical sense to me. If for some reason, a child experiences trauma, and perceives that he or she has been abandoned, even if a rational adult explains otherwise, this experience will have profound implications on the way that the child's inner mind works, and how that inner world affects the rest of the personality.

Let me explain in terms of my own life. In that hospital bed as a small child I can remember a blackness descending. It was like being suffocated by a dark, heavy, sooty mist. To counteract this, I developed an elaborate imaginary life. Inside my head I would travel on magic carpets, meet colourful and kindly characters, and spend days, whilst in that hospital bed, not being 'present' in my own body or mind. All children should be encouraged to use their imagination – it's part of what childhood is about – but I know that I used it to escape from the reality of the cold and clinical environment I found myself in; it was a coping strategy. Add to that the difficulty I had in relating to my father (to this day, I don't think he really understands why I have found life such a struggle), and you have the ingredients for problems later on.

I am not intending to 'blame' anyone, I can only write as I see and feel. It is so important to give children a positive reflection of themselves and their talents, so necessary to hold and hug a little girl, and so important to affirm her as she grows into a woman. If these things are withheld then there is often a price to pay on both sides. If the parent doesn't have the close relationship he or she wants with the child because, for whatever reason, he or she can't face their own pain, then the child tends to constantly seek approval, doesn't get enough and is then shamed for asking in the first place. The child is set up to try and find affirmation elsewhere, sometimes in inappropriate places.

Fast forward to Clare as an adult and I learned, through painful experience, that I used the same make-believe world to escape what I eventually discovered was not just plain addiction. Addiction is tough enough on its own, but it often goes hand in hand with depression. Later in life I was diagnosed with severe clinical depression and, as the professionals told me when I eventually sought help, escaping into fantasy is a common way that depressives use to try and deal with the misery. Indulging in romantic fantasy is a common way that love addicts try and escape pain. In fact, the more I used this tactic, the more obsessive I would become. Obsession is not love. It is like being in a prison, trapped by thoughts that never seem to lift except in sleep.

Of course all children, teenagers and adults have fantasies and dreams. But a non-addict or a non-depressive can recognise them as such and not spend hours dwelling in a world of her own making, or projecting into the future to such an extent that the man she has just met is the man she is sure she will marry after a five-minute conversation.

I was so shy and uncertain as a teenager. I had no idea what to do, or how to 'be' around boys, and by the time I was 14 was already developing that unhealthy obsession around food that I have already described. In a way, worrying about food was a way of 'not' worrying about the really scary stuff for a teenager – a diversionary tactic if you like. If I could blame the fact that my stomach was not as flat as I wanted it to be, then I wouldn't have to develop a healthier coping strategy. I would not have to do things the hard and embarrassing way, and learn to talk and mix with the opposite sex in the same way that everyone else had to. My family found it hard to discuss boyfriend and girlfriend-type subjects; my school was even worse. We had one biology lesson about how babies 'were made' – the teacher kept talking about newts and frogs – and the rest I learned from my friends in the playground.

The leaders of the Christian youth group that I went to did their best to explain why sexual abstinence, in their view, was what God wanted for us before we got married. But, frankly, marriage seemed a long way off at that time, and sexual feelings, like all feelings, did not just disappear because they were not acknowledged. Adolescence was a very confusing time for me, and I suppose that it was the fantasy that got me through it.

My fantasies always focused upon events outside myself. The perfect man would heal the pain. The high-profile job would take me away from the shame of not feeling good enough. More money would mean better clothes and more respect from my peers. Someone or something, one day would fix me and make everything all right. Wouldn't it?

Teenage relationships are notoriously chaotic but generally we adapt to challenges that are increasingly adult. Except that I didn't. So how was I supposed to cope with college life with the body of a young woman but the emotions of a small child?

THREE

University Challenge

'*S*o, how much did you save then?' I had been working in pubs over the summer, supposedly to save towards going to university that autumn. Unfortunately I hadn't got anything left. The excitement of having ready cash burned a hole in the pockets of my new jeans and proved to be too much of a temptation. My dad's face dropped when I told him I only had a tenner. He thrust £25 into my hot and nervous hand. My parents each gave me a kiss and helped me to carry my old duvet, a jar of coffee and a kettle into my university digs. I waved them off feeling a combination of fear, loneliness and excitement. I then ate two Mars bars in quick succession to push down the feelings.

My eating disorder kicked in, big time, during my university days. At this stage, I was merely overeating – stuffing myself with junk food, and then despising myself as I held my swollen tummy in shame. I had chosen to study drama at Manchester University; a self-conscious degree, adding even more pressure to my desire to be slim. This was the 'new romantic post punk' era. I had purple hair, long blue and pink earrings and I became a feminist overnight. I hung onto my faith proudly, though, wearing it like a trophy around my neck, arguing with my atheist tutors and students until I got the unofficial title 'token Christian'. I wasn't disliked, in fact, alongside the fervent Marxist in my tutorial group I was rather admired for being so forthright. But I used my faith as a barrier to stop anyone, man or woman, getting near me emotionally. Whilst the other drama students were having hangovers and experimenting with sex, I was hanging out with the Christian Union and performing loud and noisy street theatre at Christian student events.

Retrospectively, sexual experimentation at this stage of my life could well have been very harmful, eroding what small amount of self-esteem I possessed, and would not, I am sure, have given me the intimacy I craved. However, I know that it was as much my fear of losing control in a relationship as the Christian prohibitions about sex preached from the pulpit that prevented me from any real and honest connection with men. Much of the time I felt as though my personality was fragmented and disjointed and to compensate I played many roles – the 'wacky' drama student, the 'fervent' Christian, and at home the 'good and compliant' child.

Trying to juggle my drama life with being what I thought was a 'good Christian' at college, meant that there was almost constant tension. 'Christianity is for idiots!' was the general view from my drama friends, although they were swift to say, 'But Clare, you're not like those goody, goody God-squad people – why do you want to mix with them? They are so boring.' Most of the Christians I met were not boring at all, but it was definitely 'non-cool' to have a Christian faith and as part of my degree I studied plays that often criticised faith, the Church and all that it stood for. This made me very thoughtful, but also more anxious as I tried to imagine how to behave appropriately and to say the right thing. My fellow drama students were great fun, but they also had a reputation for being pretentious, totally self-absorbed and very judgemental. And, however much I tried, I was unable to stop bingeing on my feelings of isolation.

Trying to please both camps was impossible. Despite making some good friends, I felt almost permanently alone and I was frustrated by the compulsion to almost constantly overeat. A temporary answer came courtesy of *The Sunday Times* in 1982. The year is etched in my memory, and I can almost see the article as clearly now, over twenty years on, as I did then. It highlighted a 'dangerous' fad amongst young women, who would eat uncontrollably and then throw up to avoid weight gain. I tried it almost immediately, and was 'successful' after two or three attempts. I frequently raided my flatmates' cupboards and then threw up the contents down the loo. I kidded myself that this was a 'temporary' measure, which I would stop using when I reached my 'goal' weight.

Unfortunately, the habit became addictive. I would binge and then purge on happy or sad feelings. A play I was in went well; I would binge. A man I fancied ignored me; I would binge. Any strong feeling of any kind would prompt me to grab the biscuit tin and down its entire contents. I avoided meals out with my friends, parties and first-night drama college openings. As I became more isolated I became more depressed and more shamed, unable to tell anyone how I was feeling or what I was doing. I prayed regularly, went to Bible studies, and talked up Christianity with a fervour that would outshine the most enthusiastic preacher, but nothing could stop the behaviour.

I tentatively went to the student GP. She informed me that 'it is perfectly normal to binge and starve; let's face it, it's what our ancestors did. What you've got to try and do is just eat when you are hungry.' I didn't know what real hunger was as I made sure I never experienced it. Hunger and fear seemed to go together. And once I started eating I did not seem to able to stop. The university counsellor was more supportive and referred me to the only therapists available at the time who, when I turned up for the appointment, appeared to be in a very unorthodox relationship with each other even though they were married to other people. However, after six sessions they had unearthed the sadness I felt about the lack of connection I had with my father and they tried to explore with me why I experienced such chronic low self-esteem. I relayed a dream I'd had the night before one of my sessions: 'I am running down a white beach and a huge, kind man is waiting for me by the sea. He picks me up in his arms, holds me close and I am safe and well.' At that point I broke down in tears. The tears did not stop for two weeks. It was what I would recognise now as a minor breakdown.

Throughout those two weeks I could not understand why God would allow me to be in such pain. As I walked down Manchester's streets in the rain I thought how normal everyone else looked, and how abnormal I must be to have such a strong eating disorder grip me. I wanted the pain to stop. Thankfully, after this emotional fortnight the feelings appeared to lessen in intensity and I was able to function, go to lectures and complete my degree. It was as if they had patched me up temporarily, and the stitches were holding, for the time being anyway.

During my four years at university I could not sustain anything but severe infatuation with any of the men I felt attracted to. I remember having hysterics when one student, who I had become particularly fond of, was unavailable for the evening because he was in bed with a woman from his course. I knocked on his door to hear a muffled, 'What do you want?' and the sound of a girl laughing. I felt stupid and naive. What did I expect? I had made it clear from the start, rather pompously when

I look back on it, that I did not want or approve of sex before marriage, and although we got on famously he couldn't make any sense of my morality. He was just doing what many students do, getting drunk, having sex and thinking about the consequences later.

Even then I remember feeling that if this student would whisk me away on a fictitious white charger, then all would be well; I would be safe and both of us would live in harmony in some pink cloud paradise. I wanted to be Barbie to his Ken except, as always, I never felt good enough or thin enough. At alcohol-fuelled evenings in nightclubs I was always stone cold sober. I did not want to lose control, I compared my body to the other girls, and I despaired of ever having a flat stomach or the 'right' figure. I was not fat but I thought I was and that all my 'problems' would be solved if I was thinner and more attractive. I also had a totally unrealistic understanding of what a genuine relationship really entailed. Pia Mellody, an author and counsellor who has specialised in the area of love addiction puts it this way:

> A love addict is someone who is dependent on, enmeshed with, and compulsively focused on taking care of another person ... not all love addicts are co-dependent but they can be. Co-dependence is a disease of immaturity caused by childhood trauma. Co-dependents are immature and childish to such a degree that the condition hampers their life.[1]

Throughout my student years, I discovered Christians who were kind and understanding about the sense of isolation I felt, but I could never bring myself to tell them directly about the bulimia. Nowadays, eating disorders are discussed far more openly, but 20 years ago they were not, and so the shame I felt was immense. I would cry myself to sleep at night, thinking that if I could find someone to love me enough then all the pain would go. I was envious of my flatmates' boyfriends and friendships and although they did their best to reassure me that 'there was someone out there for me' I never really believed them and resigned myself to a life of sad and desperate singleness.

Eventually the white knight did appear, in the shape of my ex-husband. The fear I'd felt for so many years temporarily subsided. I could not believe that someone would want to marry me. And my logic said, 'If he loves me, then surely I must love him back; after all I might never get another chance?'

The night he proposed I had prepared dinner. The recipe for chicken in double cream (I was horrified by how fattening this was) came from the *Slut's Cookbook*, a present from my mother because of my lack of ability in the kitchen. The cream curdled, and as I tried to cover it up with parsley I felt sick with excitement and fear. I knew he was planning to ask me the big question – I just wasn't sure when. He was everything I could have wanted: kind, supportive, good-looking, a great listener and a Christian. 'So he must be the one mustn't he? God wouldn't have brought him into my life otherwise,' went my logic. I loved him as much as I was able to love any-one at the time. I was pathetically grateful for his regard and we had much in common.

The 'but' came from a female vicar friend who gently tried to push me off my fluffy cloud and remind me of my age (I was 23) and inexperience with men. 'Are you sure; really sure? Why not wait another year and see?' He had actually half proposed a year earlier anyway, and the thought of losing him if I said 'no' this time felt unbearable. Nothing compared with the great high of being loved and cherished by another human being, as I had no idea how to cherish myself. I decided to say 'yes' because to say 'no' would have left me utterly bereft. My thoughts were unwittingly selfish – I can see that now. They centred on how I felt, what he would bring to my life, how safe and secure I felt. I am sure that I had many qualities that he appreciated, but I assumed that he was doing me the favour, rescuing me from all the pain and food chaos.

He certainly put up with my neurosis around eating. I would get very anxious about going out to dinner and I would make mental calculations about how many calories I consumed. If a restaurant didn't have low-fat salads on the menu, I didn't want to know, and I would be terrified of meeting friends in their homes, as I could not control what I was given to eat. I was clearly a very cheap date! Although the bulimia eased off as my emptiness was filled, at least temporarily, by the extraordinary sense of being the focus of his attention, I was constantly dieting, starving and/or bingeing and always on the scales. There is a tyranny about addiction that the sufferer cannot see; it affects families, husbands, wives, partners and whole families. The addict's behaviour can become the focus of so much, not leaving much space for others' needs and concerns. I can only suppose that he was drawn to me because of a familiarity he felt from somewhere in his past. I know I was drawn to him because of the utter security I felt he gave me, and the overwhelming kindness he displayed whenever I was angry, upset or desperate.

I am not sure I knew who he really was at all. That's the trouble with self- obsession born of unresolved pain; it stops us from really 'seeing' people as they are. That so-called 'perfect partner' becomes a projection of what we want them to be and then we become resentful when they don't live up to those unrealistic expectations, which no human being can. That resentment then erodes the relationship; it breaks up, and those feelings of abandonment and despair come back with a vengeance, prompting the search for another 'perfect' partner to fill the void. The cycle goes on and on unless it's broken.

I cannot presume to know his feelings now about our marriage and its break-up. That is his business. Neither do I want to punish myself for the decision to marry when I was clearly so immature. I have been hard enough on myself already. Apart from the fact that I was a 15-year-old in a 23-year-old body – eating disorders tend to prevent those suffering from emotionally maturing – I was also heavily influenced by the Christians I knew at the time. There was great pressure on me to marry whilst still a virgin, and there was always someone who would back this view up with a hefty dose of biblical justification. I had strong sexual feelings, so surely this meant marriage or nothing? I wonder whether God is as obsessed with genital activity as our society appears to be, Christian or otherwise? I am not promoting promiscuity or sex as recreation, I just wonder about the number of other relationships that may have moved faster than they should have done due to that kind of pressure.

I left university, we married, and I began my determined climb up the media ladder, feeling whole at last, and grateful that this relationship seemed to scare the bulimic side of me away. But of course, things are never so simple, and although the pain had eased it had not been erased, since its root cause had never really been addressed.

FOUR

Career and Cravings

$\mathcal{M}$y career and my work have always been areas where I have been in the driving seat. From as early as I can remember I longed to work in radio. At the age of 12 I would listen to *Anna and the Doc*, a problem-solving talk show on London's Capital Radio, and wonder whether I could ever be the host of a programme like that. It was a live phone-in with anyone calling about anything. The calls went something like this: Peter from Croydon, 'Anna, I want to break up with my girlfriend, but I don't know how.' Emma from Shepherd's Bush, 'I am worried because I haven't got my periods yet, and I am 15,' and so on. The presenter, Sarah Ward, was and is a bit of a hero of mine, and when I eventually got to work with her in the late 1980s it seemed, on the surface, as though I had realised one of my dreams.

'Thank you for joining us, and now, here's the travel.' I loved my first local radio job in Nottingham. As a new BBC recruit I looked after *The Golden Years: Music from the 40s and 50s*, presented by a man with no teeth, and I had my own music request show at weekends. It was a rude awakening for my faith. 'How can you be a Christian and not be an idiot?' my first BBC boss asked. 'Nearly didn't give you the job, but you were too entertaining to turn down!' We made a deal. If he stopped banging on about Marxism, then I wouldn't beat him up with a Bible. He turned into a great friend.

Live broadcasting became my next real obsession and the next few years were spent focusing on my career. I fretted over jobs, competed for better ones, and learned how to be a half decent radio journalist. Although work boosted my self-esteem, I became so absorbed in it that I almost 'became' my job. I loved broadcasting, partly because it was something I could do well – I can talk for Britain, and to do so gave me a great 'high', I had lots of laughs and it took me away from the feelings of in-security and worthlessness. Being on the end of that microphone, debating anything from dog dirt on the streets to dodgy car sales techniques was a real privilege and a good learning ground. Sadly, my career could not 'cure' the bulimia, which returned with a vengeance just a few years into my marriage.

During the mid-1980s I had moved to London tem-porarily with the BBC, and was commuting home to Nottingham to be with my husband at the weekends. I am sure it was a lonely existence for him but for me, at first, it was compelling and exciting. I then left that BBC job to start as an Editor and Presenter at Capital Radio but very quickly I felt out of my depth. The salary was good and the people were talented and determined, and even though I put on a good show, I felt overwhelmed and afraid. My insecurity drove me to prove myself, and I felt that asking for help would be an admission of weakness. I was deeply bulimic at this time, and I would binge and purge in my rented room in central London. The loneliness I felt was overwhelming and I would try and block it out with food and by working ever harder. One minute I would be interviewing pop icons, the next politicians. It was a great gig. But emotionally I was not up to it. The strain was overwhelming and I hoped that my flatmate couldn't hear me when I used the bathroom after the binges. The days became more and more of a struggle and I eventually resigned from the Capital job, returning north to find work that was more manageable. I was deeply frustrated by my inability to cope with the pressure and to pass up such a good career move. I didn't want to leave, but I had become physically and emotionally exhausted. After many tears and much soul searching I managed to find another job with the BBC nearer home in Birmingham.

I felt a great sense of failure as I watched many of my Capital colleagues go on to grander and greater things. Looking back now, I doubt I was emotionally strong enough to cope with any more pressure, but at the time I felt I had let down my family and myself. There was no doubt that I could broadcast. Radio, to this day, is my first love, but I did not have the inner strength then to cope with the insecurity of the profession, the back-biting and the knowledge that I was only as good as the last programme I hosted or planned. Truthfully, others were much more generous towards me than I was towards myself, but I could not see that. All I wanted was to be perfect immediately because I believed that if I wasn't, I would be sacked and ultimately abandoned, left to rot in the slow lane. Of course, I did not realise that I was constantly abandoning myself, over and over again.

Inevitably my eating disorder affected my marriage, and the commuting backwards and forwards to London had not helped. My poor husband never knew what kind of a wife he was returning home to at the end of the day. Would she be upbeat and positive? Or would she be depressed, bloated with excess food and unable to get out of bed? Frankly, I am amazed he stuck by me for as long as he did. We hit rock bottom many times. He used to say, 'When the relationship is good, it's great. When it's not, it's just awful.' I had no sense of what nurturing a relationship meant, as I had no sense of being able to nurture myself; the state of our relationship was dictated by the state of my mental health. A kind of unintended tyranny on my part, I suppose.

Reluctantly I began therapy again with the wife of the vicar at our local church. The first session was a shock but enlightening. 'Lie down', she told me 'and imagine you are in the loo. Now think of flowers coming from the loo instead of using it to be sick. Now what do you feel?' Frankly, I felt daft. It was a tentative, but strange, beginning. But the relief I got by telling her about my illness was immense. She prayed for me, and we explored some of the possible reasons behind the behaviour – the childhood hospital experience and the loneliness I felt when I was younger. I was, though, at this point, losing patience with God, as I had now been 'ill' for nearly five years and there seemed to be no way out of the cycle. I recall a friend praying over me asking for the 'spirit' of bulimia to leave me, but nothing happened and I began to despair that things would ever change.

We eventually moved from the Midlands to London, and both found work. I landed a job on the breakfast programme, GMTV. This brought with it hopes that perhaps this time I could beat my eating problem, become famous and find happiness. I made a name for myself as a funny and creative reporter. One Christmas, the editor gave me a fairy outfit. 'Put that on,' he commanded. 'I want you to wave your magic wand and report from a Christmas tree forest, in the snow, tomorrow morning. If you can climb a tree, and do it from there, all the better. And make us laugh!' Desperate to go to the loo before my 'bit', I remember crouching in a blizzard and asking the cameraman to, 'Tell base I am peeing. I am not ready to present!' It was fun, but very stressful too, with a real emphasis on the right looks and the right clothes. After the initial euphoria of this new job wore off, I returned to bingeing and purging and each episode was worse than the last. It was the same story every time I moved location or got a new position. The eating disorder would ease for a few weeks and then, when the novelty wore off, I would be back to square one.

I see now that this pattern of behaviour is common to all addicts. Whether its relationships, work, shopping, drugs or booze, we will use anything and everything to avoid our feelings. Deal with one addiction and the chances are that the problem will emerge, like a bulge in a bunged-up pipe, somewhere else. Feeling desperate on the bus after a gruelling 12-hour night shift one morning, I read of a treatment centre that claimed to specialise in helping those suffering from eating disorders. I rang them immediately and booked an assessment with the therapist.

'All I want is to beat this eating disorder and get on with the rest of my life.' That's what I said at my first session. If only it had been that simple. But I was very ignorant about addiction in those days, and I sincerely believed that a quick fix from the right head doctor would do the trick. My first appointment was terrifying; I carried so much fear with me wherever I went. I was worried about saying the 'wrong' thing. I was frightened that the therapist would tell me that my faith was the cause of all the problems. I was concerned that I would be sectioned, have tubes put in my arm, and not let out of hospital until I was well. My fears were groundless. The therapist was sympathetic and kind, and she asked questions that were perceptive, knowledgeable and helpful. She recommended that I eat three balanced meals a day, excluding sugar and white flour as these tended to be my binge foods. I reluctantly agreed to book five more sessions, but I did not turn up for all of them as I was so ashamed about needing therapy in the first place. I wanted to just 'get on with it'; I didn't want to navel-gaze and be one of those inadequate people who couldn't sort out their own problems.

It took about a year for me to be able to eat properly without the bulimia kicking in. Each meal was an ordeal. 'How much potato should I have? Will this meat mean I put on weight? What if I lose control? How much bread is too much?' Very slowly my brain and body adjusted to the new routine, and I thought I was 'cured'. But of course I had really only begun to heal. When, years later, I left my marriage hoping, self-indulgent though this may sound, to 'find myself' – and then found myself unable to exist without a man – I discovered a whole new set of challenges and a whole new level of despair. The craving for food mirrored my deeper craving: for love. Briar Whitehead's book of the same name, *Craving for Love*, describes the dilemma perfectly:

> We relationship addicts will resist the idea that our relationships are unhealthy, simply because we cannot do without them: they are our source of life and love. We (develop) elaborate, even scriptural justifications for them. We cannot stop our manner of relating anyway, no matter how much we try. The Christian relationship addict has probably done everything she knows to rid her life of 'sin' – in the absence of any understanding of the true nature of pain.[1]

Towards the end of my marriage, and frequently after the divorce, the same therapist suggested that I try a Twelve Step fellowship as a way of dealing with my addictive behaviour. These fellowships were a turning point for me, in a whole range of ways. But it took at least two years before I was ready to really participate, and it was only when the pain got bad enough that I was prepared to follow her advice.

My 'will' and the way it manifested itself in my work was strong, but I had learned, up to this point anyway, that if I tried hard enough I would normally succeed. I rationalised this determination as one of the God-given cards that I had been dealt (and in later years have put to better use) and I was normally in such a rush to find the next job and the next promotion that I did not sit back and consider whether it would be nurturing and fulfilling. Such is the compulsion of the addict who is constantly running and trying to prove that he/she is good enough. I would bore my husband to death with the ins and outs of my working week. 'I did this interview, it went well, but I don't think I covered x, y or z properly ... what do you think?' Or, 'I hate editing. I can't do it, I can't tell other people what to do. I don't know what stories to cover!' And so it went on. At the weekends I would sleep forever, and there was no time to invest in friendships, my marriage or any hobbies. Anyway, weren't hobbies for the bored and unfulfilled? I wasn't one of those sad individuals. I had the job, my eating disorder and enough money to buy clothes when and where I wanted to and that, even though I had stirrings that there might be a bigger picture, was what I thought living was all about.

I am a firm believer that God only give us as much as we can cope with. The depression I have suffered in more recent years would have, at this stage, been impossible for me to have faced since I had too many layers to delve down into before I really faced that darkness and isolation.

During our early days in London I would pay lipservice, in church services or in home group Bible meetings to 'letting God's will be done'. I would bow my head and pray fervently, 'God, I know you want what's best for me, but if I could get this job/promotion/TV appearance, then I know I would be happy.' In reality, I hadn't really got a clue what 'God's will' meant. The wounded child within naturally assumed, because of my distorted understanding of God, that my will would always be opposed to his. I grasped that I had skills that possibly could be applied to bigger and more prestigious broadcasting jobs, but if I didn't get the TV job that I auditioned for or the grand radio presenting job that I had set my heart on, I felt let down and ignored by the creator, as if he was personally 'making me learn a lesson'. This in turn reinforced the belief that I did not feel that I deserved any success unless I proved that I was holy or faithful enough.

Full-on household-name success has always eluded me, thank God! I could do without all those worries about body image, privacy and press intrusion. Yet, Big Brother-like, deep down, I thought that fame and its partner, fortune, would be the thing that would solve all my woes.

There is a part of me, and I think that I am like most people in this, that would like recognition for what I think I do well, but I have almost lost that craving for public recognition. I say, almost, as I am still human, I have an ego, and I am still quite capable of indulging my vanity and showing off. How bizarre to believe that you can get enough love from 'them out there' when you haven't worked out how to access it inside. To have my value defined by how well-known I am is fickle and dangerous, but if I am honest, it was what I desired in my early career.

Sometimes I feel it is a double whammy being a recovering addict and having a Christian faith. I have described, as I see it, my struggle to 'let go' of control on a daily basis and to 'let God', as the saying goes, but when it comes to compulsion and its relationship with my faith things become more complex.

As I mentioned at the start of the book, it is no good telling an alcoholic, a compulsive overeater, an anorexic, a bulimic or a drug addict to just 'stop' using. In fact it is almost insulting. Most smokers will tell you how many times they tried and then gave in to the craving. Will-power does not work, precisely because the behaviour is about other things. Addictions are the tip of the iceberg, masking feelings that are not being felt, sexual desires that are repressed, and painful pasts that have not been acknowledged. No one really knows why some can walk away from drugs, compulsive sexual or romantic behaviour, or overeating and why others can't. Sometimes maturity means we grow out of self-destructive behaviours. We find that when an underlying depression is properly addressed, those behaviours can also diminish and ultimately disappear. For the addict, though, willpower is the enemy. It is admitting powerlessness over the behaviour that, ironically, proves to be so empowering.

After our move to London, and the meeting with the therapist there, I continued to explore how my childhood affected my life at that point, I examined some of the fear behind the need to control my food and, most significantly of all, I asked questions about my marriage. I have heard many Christians express concern that therapy leads to relationship break-ups. I don't believe that. If there are problems that exist, they will emerge anyway, and that's what happened to me. I cannot speak for my ex-husband, as I believe he did all he could to keep our relationship working. For my part, I felt as if I had married young, not knowing who or what I was, and although I loved him as far as I was capable, I came to the realisation that I had expected him to meet all my needs as I had never learned to meet them for myself. That, of course, is a huge pressure on any individual; no one can or should have to live up to those kinds of expectations. He never wanted a separation, but I became convinced that this was the only way for me to heal and grow. I had no idea how hard the path I had chosen would be.

FIVE

Single Again

$\mathcal{S}$itting in my rented flat, the silence seemed to ricochet off the walls. 'What have I done?' I asked myself over and over again. 'I had the love of a good man, and now I have thrown it all away. For what – a rented flat and swathes of loneliness?' I sat, surrounded by boxes and Kleenex, unpacking and crying at the same time. Of course I regretted my decision, but I could not see how I could stay in the relationship and discover who I was. Sadly, I seemed to lose all those friends who had known me as a married woman. I felt let down at the time, but I realised it was not malice on their part; half of them just did not know where I had gone. I was grateful for support whenever it came. My female vicar friend helped me out on moving-house day, and one other good friend proved to be indispensable.

She was not someone I had met in church circles, but an old acquaintance from my days on the radio in the Midlands. She was loyal, loving and totally accepting of my situation. I shall always be grateful to her and her partner for their love and support. I used to get through each day, if I was not working, by going to the shops and chatting to a shop assistant – that way I felt I was still part of the human race. My family were great, and although they didn't know all the ins and outs of my hardship, they were always there to help me if I needed them. My mother visited my rented flat in central

43

London and stayed one weekend. I remember her cooking me an omelette on my small kitchen stove; possibly the only good meal that I had that week. One thing I began to learn as I started the painful and slow road to proper recovery is how much I need other people and how necessary and normal that support is. But my fear of being controlled by others has meant it has taken years to get to the stage of asking for that kind of encouragement.

Ironically, my career had picked up just as my relationship had gone down the pan, although that upturn was not going to last. Incredibly, I had managed to land myself a very prestigious job, as a reporter for Channel 4 News. I dragged myself in for the first day, dreading the stress that I thought would lie ahead. Not the attitude best suited to starting a new role. 'Let's look at natural birth control gadgets,' said my editor. 'Clare, you can get on to it.' Dutifully I researched the story and produced a report that became the lead later in the week; a great success then? That's not what I felt at all. I would find my mind drifting off in planning meetings, distracted by the wedding rings on the hands of my colleagues. I frequently went to the loo to weep out of fear and self-loathing. What was I trying to prove? I felt so fragile that I don't know how I survived the five months I was there. Everyone was kind and compassionate; amazing, when I think how newsrooms can be, full of testosterone and aggression. Eventually, though, I just could not cope. I knew I needed the money, but I also knew I was breaking up inside. I decided to leave.

I felt so ashamed when I handed in my notice to the editor. It felt like the Capital Radio experience some years earlier. I told my boss that I had been offered work in Chicago, which was not untrue, but it was not the main reason that I quit. I felt that if I told him the truth I would be judged and labelled 'unreliable', so I left, trying to hold my head up high, but inside feeling a complete failure. On my last day, I went through the process of being cheery at my leaving do, and when I got home, I broke down. The idea of praying at this time was not something I felt I was worthy to do, as I felt sure that God would not 'approve' of someone who had initiated the breakup of a Christian marriage. 'Please help me, Father,' was about all I was capable of asking through tears of sadness and shame.

To be truthful, I think subconsciously I had wanted to get off the media treadmill for some time but I wanted to do it in my own time, not someone else's. I was also facing a financial abyss. How on earth was I going to pay my rent, buy food and simply survive on the limited savings I had when there was no money coming in?

In the month that followed I was in a state of complete panic. One day I was so distraught I dropped to my knees and asked for God's help. 'Please sort this out,' I pleaded. 'I need work, I need a place to go in the day, and I need it soon.' Bizarrely the phone went and it was Channel 4's political editor. 'Would you consider reporting two days a week on our lunchtime political programme? I think you would be great!' Would I consider it? I accepted like a shot and with that break I was able to get other work to fit around it. That – even I realised – was an answer to prayer.

Even though my confidence was at rock bottom and another relationship was the last thing I needed, I felt I should try and make the effort to 'get out there, and get on with my life'. It would have been better to face my grief first. In fact, getting to grips with my aloneness was one of the reasons I left my marriage. But without many friendships and only one therapy session a week, that task seemed insurmountable and I began to look for a boyfriend. I started to train for the London Marathon as a way of meeting people and getting out of my lonely flat. Exercise seemed to dull the pain and in the pub one night I noticed an attractive and friendly man who, amazingly enough, seemed interested in me. I felt it was love at first running workout. What I was actually doing was projecting all my hopes of being 'saved' onto this poor human man, and hoping he would live up to my totally unrealistic expectations.

For non-addicts, dating and exploring other relationships probably appears to be normal behaviour. But for me, it was running away from a perceived abyss. I was trying to fill the hole in my soul the only way I knew how.

Pulled muscles, stinking trainers and sweaty armpits don't traditionally prompt romance but we managed to get together just the same. By focusing on another human being I did not have to focus on myself. When that ended, I vowed I would stay single until I had processed my grief and discovered a little bit more about who I was. But the fear became too great and I embarked on another liaison that produced great highs and great lows.

What I am about to write is not easy, but I feel that unless I am totally honest I would be doing myself, and you, a disservice. When I clapped eyes on my next prospective romance, it was as though I had been struck by a oversized four-wheeled SUV. He was broad-shouldered, handsome and very, very funny. I fell in love or at least, in lust, instantly. This was passion that came with a price. When we first met I had no idea that he was already attached – he chose not to mention that in our early encounters. By the time I discovered that he already had a partner and a child, I was hooked. We had an affair for two years.

I also discovered much later, after he had left his partner, that he had in fact been married to his ex. How he could have kept this a secret shows up the madness of an addicted relationship. The marriage bombshell came on a summer holiday. Sitting at dinner in the sun in Majorca with his closest friends, I chatted to their eldest daughter. 'I was the flower girl at his wedding,' she said, unaware of the consequences. 'What wedding?' I replied, in shock. She was mortified, I was very upset, and my boyfriend looked sheepish. I stood up, rushed to the loo, wept and rang a girlfriend. Later, when all the hysterics had subsided, I began to look at my part in this drama.

Of course he should not have lied, but he said how hard it was to talk to me about his previous relationship as I was inclined to fly off the handle and become irrational. Although it was incredibly painful for me to discover this 'secret' in such a bizarre way, I do know that I have a part to play as well. Perhaps I am not always the gentle, loving Clare that I want the world to see? Perhaps I, too, am capable of tyranny, great anger and rage? That re-evaluation is freeing. It allows me to acknowledge the darker sides of my personality rather than pretend that they are not there. Then I can become more whole, and then I can even forgive those who hurt me. I am no longer the victim, having to blame everyone else for my misfortune. I, too, am flawed and I don't have to make everyone else 'wrong' to make myself 'right'. Whether I would have walked away from this relationship earlier had I known he was married, I cannot say. I think it would have made a difference, but I did not have the full information so I could not make that choice. Of course I realise that my behaviour was wrong. I was extremely depressed at this time, and I could well have done with some psychiatric help, but I was too proud and too frightened to pursue that path.

The life of the 'other woman' is full of drama, intensity and excitement. It also produces suicidal lows, terrible guilt, lonely weekends and public holidays, and the kind of despair from which there seems no escape.

There were passionate 'I love you, and I want to be with you' emails, secret meetings in romantic London locations, and bagfuls of love letters. Thankfully this was before texting became the norm, as the phone bills would have been enormous.

I took holidays alone, trying to forget him. Sitting on a bench in Gozo, an island off Malta, I wept as looked out at the sea and the small ships, their lights glinting on the water. A monk, who was on holiday and who probably could have done without being interrupted by a woman who had mascara running down her face, sat next to me. Before I knew it I had told him about the affair and he kindly looked at me and said, in broken English, 'Remember the prodigal son. Nothing you have done is impossible for God to forgive.' That has always stayed with me, although it didn't change my actions on my return to the UK.

After several bouts of hysterics on my part, and much deliberation on his, he left his partner, both of us ready to sail off into the sunset. Although we hoped we would live happily ever after, the reality was very different. His and my guilt, my depression and our mutual neediness, prompted terrible arguments, dramatic rows and endless fights and reconciliations. We did not live together which, in retrospect, was a blessing, as it gave us both time to reflect on what we were doing and where we were trying to go. I knew deep down that I had much work to do on myself. Add to that the constant guilt that I had about this man leaving his family and, as you can imagine, this was hardly a union made in heaven. However, the prospect of letting another man go, and having to face that yawning lonely gulf, was far more frightening, never mind the self-loathing I felt at hurting another woman and child. Believe me, I will go to my grave with that, but I literally felt I would die if I left him, or if he left me. I am not attempting to justify the behaviour but just to tell it how it was.

He, of course, had choices too, so it was not all one way, but I felt the weight of God's possible retribution heavily and the shame was overwhelming. There are many who might say that if we 'pulled ourselves together' and put aside our own selfish needs we would be able to make the right moral choices, but in the addictive realm, choice does not really enter in to it. It is as if you have no control and no autonomy.

Throughout this time I talked to God, and could only find solace in Catholic churches due, I think, to my unfamiliarity with this tradition. Church communities that reminded me of my evangelical past prompted panic attacks and sheer terror and I would have to leave, staggering outside to gasp for air, fearing God's judgement as well as judgement from those I was supposed to be worshipping alongside. In these churches everyone seemed to be happily married with beautiful children, large cars, and larger houses with accessories to match. In London's Catholic cathedral I found I felt most at ease alongside the homeless alcoholics who came and sat next to me to escape the cold in London's Victoria Street. My compulsions were like theirs; I felt I was among exiles and friends. We would speak sometimes after the Mass. They would slur and sway and I would cry and talk gibberish. On occasions we would hug each other, clumsily and awkwardly, their street smell lingering on my clothes long after the service had ended.

During the time this boyfriend and I were together I felt increasingly lost and disorientated, and as a result we must have split up nearly a dozen times. Each time that we separated, however, the anxiety got too great and the relationship resumed. Although he had his issues, and he did not want to look at them, he was not to blame. In fact, I genuinely loved him, and I simply expected him to be a kind of divine solution, to meet all my needs and make me happy. I suspect he felt the same. I hadn't learned to meet those needs myself, so he was on a no-win ticket. Although we had many good times, and he tried his utmost to be everything I wanted, it was never enough, because I believed I was never enough.

I began to realise that there might be something wrong with me. I can hear you saying, 'Began to realise! How long does it take, woman?' It was as if this person was a drug I simply could not put down. When we split up, for what I thought was the final time, the grief was overwhelming, and there seemed to be no way I could process it. Each day was like walking through black treacle, with no joy, no hope and no prospect of improvement.

I later discovered that this feeling of alienation and despair was a kind of withdrawal, similar to that experienced by a drug addict or alcoholic when they first try to get clean. Coincidentally, I lost a prestigious radio job, so I was forced to face myself without the luxury of work to distract me. I swore and cursed at God. 'Thanks,' I said, 'no job, no relationship, overwhelming feelings of sadness 24/7 and no money either. This is just perfect.' Losing everything in order to gain true life is not something I had truly ever grasped. It sounded rather austere and punishing to me. Paying lip-service to biblical phrases is one thing; experiencing their reality is completely different. 'Lose everything, God. No thanks! I'm fine.' Except that I wasn't.

Addiction, of course takes many forms. I have always been driven in my work, and a bit of a 'shopaholic'. Both these behaviours can be indicative of an addictive personality. Addiction is a 'clever disease and it will emerge anywhere at any time. 'I shop, therefore I am' is a modern mantra, and humans are positively encouraged to work themselves into early graves in the belief that this is somehow noble and desirable. 'God helps those who help themselves!' I've no idea where that phrase comes from, but I hate it for its smugness and accusatory tone.

In my work I was always driven to climb an imaginary ladder, although once I got up to the next rung I always focused on the one above. After leaving Channel 4, I freelanced and just about managed to make ends meet. Then I landed a demanding talk radio breakfast show in London that I hosted for a year. After 12 months I was shocked to discover I was to be replaced by a talented male celebrity. I remember the conversation with my boss when he told me that there 'was no place for me on the radio station, as we are going in a different direction'.

I broke down and wept, clutching a bit of BBC loo roll from the desk in his office, saying, 'I am 40, what will I do now? How will I earn? Where do I go?' With hindsight, this job loss was the start of a much more creative approach to my life and my career, although at the time it was excruciatingly painful.

I bear the BBC boss no resentment whatsoever. Presenting is an insecure profession and most people in this field will be fired at some time, but the loss of my well-paid, high-status job was a huge shock to my ego, my income and my stability. For three months afterwards I lived on the redundancy pay, unsure of what my next move should be. Prompted initially by my (at that point) ex-boyfriend, and also by a deep longing within, I decided to explore the possibility of further study, in theology at King's College in London.

I am always amazed at how God works, and I was fortunate to meet with the University's Dean in order to discuss the possibility of further study. He was kind, non-judgmental and wise. I took my desire to read theology as part of a possible first step towards ordination, although there was a voice in my head that continually said, 'What, *you*, a relationship breaker, a *priest!*' In fact, you may well be thinking, 'What on earth!', but the thought of ordination has honestly always been a niggle. Many of my friends had always joked about me being a vicar and I took this as confirmation that I was meant to pursue this path and this 'higher purpose' for the next few years of my life. I realise now how much I need to hide behind prestigious labels. The apparent nobility of the ordination path somehow assuaged my guilt (temporarily of course) about the affair in the past, and full of fervour and endeavour I embarked upon the course.

I began combining studying with some shift work I had managed to get on a television news programme. I hated the work. I found it degrading and exhausting. My bosses were bright and feisty, most of them a good ten years younger than me. I resented their apparent confidence when I felt so much on my uppers. I felt as though I had blown my career and I hated scrimping and saving for food and cheap clothes.

On the way to each shift I would talk myself into it, saying, 'Think about the money, think about the money,' in the hope that I could psyche myself into a more positive mood. During the exhausting and long night shifts I got to know my fellow workers, but I had a deep resentment towards the work I was doing; it felt beneath me. However, I could justify it to myself by loftily proclaiming my commitment to my degree, and seeing it as a means to an end. My pride was clearly taking a huge bashing, possibly not before time.

One of the presenters from my former radio station bumped into me in the newsroom corridor and sneered in front of my fellow journalists, 'O how the mighty have fallen!' I remember the shame and embarrassment I felt, how much I missed the identity of being a 'presenter', and how hard it was to work with the back-room boys because I needed the money. All that seems achingly vain now, but at the time it felt as though my professional world, at least, had ended.

I look back at that job now as a strange gift. I had more honest conversations about my struggles and my faith with my colleagues in the early hours of the morning than I had had for many years, and even though the work was draining, the friendships could be nourishing and satisfying. As many of my co-workers knew I was thinking of becoming a priest I was asked all kinds of questions in the small hours. 'My father's dying, and I need to talk about it,' was one discussion I had with a colleague. I was asked by another for 'good bits' in the Bible for weddings, and I also shared some of my own struggles with addiction and relationships. It was the best and worst of times.

My degree, too, in the long term, added to my under-standing of God's love for me, opening up a whole new world of understanding that deepened my faith. The course also brought me into contact with some wonder-ful people, asking similar questions and going through similar challenges. There was the mature student who was top of our class. By day she worked at Tesco, and by night she studied, simultaneously raising her child as a single parent. Like me, she juggled her shifts to get to lectures. I did not feel alone when it came to leading an exhausting and complicated life!

The Dean suggested that I attend an 'ordination week-end' to explore my supposed 'calling' to priesthood. My boyfriend (we were together at this time) kindly came with me, and it was as much of a culture shock to me as it was to him. Our leader was an RAF pilot turned Christian worker, and with great honesty and courage he talked of his own struggles, doubts and fears in relation to his faith.

Everyone around us seemed to be young, fully clued up

about the whole process, and incredibly spiritual about the journey they felt they were embarking upon. One wannabe ordinand looked at me with great sincerity during a meal and asked whether I had 'been doing the Lord's work for long?' I nearly spat out my over-cooked Brussels sprout. I have never done Christian lingo very well as I think it sometimes doesn't mean much to those who are 'outside the club'. However, I managed a stilted reply along the lines of, 'If the Lord will have me, I'll do whatever work he wants,' and the conversation went dead.

I remember feeling terribly disorientated and very grateful that I was not on my own in such a 'Christian' environment. However, when I asked in a session whether 'anyone else was like me and really struggled with believing that God heard them, or even at times doubted whether God even existed' I got nothing but positive feedback. It turns out that many others felt the same, but were too afraid to voice their fears. However, the old terrors of not being good enough and panic reappeared, and I really began to wonder whether this 'priest thing' was for me.

I have always felt much more at home in my working journalist environment than I ever have in any overtly Christian situation. My instinct tells me that even though the faithful appear to be genuine, real feelings can sometimes be glossed over in spiritual language. Emotions such as anger, resentment, sexual desire, jealousy and fury are so well hidden that I often wonder whether I inhabit the same universe as those around me. At least in a newsroom people are openly competitive, out to get the story, and hugely ambitious, and I know what I am dealing with! That is, of course, a generalisation and I am thankful that my experience at King's College brought me into contact with some wonderful and obviously human Christian individuals, allowing me to feel right at home.

Single Again

During my second year at King's College I was still free-lancing in TV and radio, juggling my studies with working and becoming more and more exhausted. I was also becoming more and more depressed, and I could not recognise the symptoms. Yes, the affair boyfriend and I had split up again (!) and the loneliness of not being in a relationship turned from a deep sadness to a suicidal despair. I must sound like a human yo-yo, going in and out of this relationship, but that is the madness of addictive behaviour, repeating the same behaviour over and over again, each time expecting a different outcome. 'This time it will be different,' says the alcoholic. 'Just one drink won't hurt.' 'Just one more binge will make me feel better,' says the anorexic and bulimic, 'and then I'll stop.' 'We can work out this partnership this time, as I really feel I have changed,' says the relationship addict. 'After all, I know him/her so well.' It is a cycle of despair, denial and shame, getting worse and worse with each 'hit'.

I felt a sense of deep failure at my inability to hold down a successful relationship and get myself a satisfying job when everyone around me appeared to be in happy stable partnerships, getting on with their lives and having some laughs along the way. I was in my early forties, with a cat and a small flat, and I felt as though I had achieved nothing.

At night, in the oppressive blackness of my small bedroom, the words 'you are pointless, useless and hopeless' would ricochet around my mind like a mantra. I would lie awake in tears and in panic, waking every day at 4am. I cried before I went to work and when I got home. This was definitely a depressive episode, but I thought I was simply stressed and grieving. It got worse and worse. Each day was harder than the next. The critical chatter in my exhausted brain got louder and I began to feel as though I could not live much longer like this, but I did not know what to do next.

Temporary relief came completely unexpectedly. In retrospect, what followed was prompted by years of unresolved grief over previous relationships as much as the need to find the next fix. I was still doing the gruelling night shifts, and trying to study for my theology finals.

I began what was initially an innocent email conversation with a friend of a friend; I was simply after some functional information. Emails and texts are the love addicts' premium five-star fuel, and I began to live in a fictitious fantasy world, wondering what he was like and whether he was single. I can see now that I was running away from all the uncomfortable feelings I could not face due to my sadness at the past and the terror of a possible lonely and desolate future.

The emails started something like this:

Send to: R
Subject matter: Address please
Hallo, do you have the mail address of xxxx as I need to get in touch with him? My name is Clare and I am doing a Theology diploma at King's. I think I met you some years ago at some conference or another. I hope this is ok?

Fast-forward to roughly four weeks later and the emails ended up something like this:

Send to: Clare Catford
Subject matter: Re: address
I have deep feelings for you, although my partner and I have a confusing relationship as you know. I am married but ...

I now believe, and I am actually no cynic, that this is a common ailment affecting many partnered men; the 'I am married but ... ' syndrome. Any of the following phrases will finish the sentence: 'I am married but ... '

'my wife doesn't understand me', 'my wife and I don't have sex anymore', 'ever since we have had children we are no longer close', 'she prefers her friends to me', 'we lead separate lives', and so on. Pick the appropriate phrase and stick it into the sentence and it all means the same. 'I am not happy, I am not prepared to do anything about it, so how about an affair that will take me away from having to face my own stuff?'

I had not twigged the 'I am married but ... ' syndrome at this stage and obviously it took a great deal of email correspondence to get from 'A' to 'B', but I could feel my brain fizzing with the intrigue and mystery. I was taking part in my own low-grade Catherine Cookson novel, updated for the twenty-first century.

In emails we both shared inappropriate revelations about our past lives and current feelings. He told me about the hiccups in his marriage, I told him about the huge highs and lows in my own relationships. It was compelling at first, erotically charged and great fun. Nothing was off-limits. Sex, resentments, and angry dialogues – the conversations were entirely without any healthy boundaries or limits. I have had subsequent email connections that have been much more controlled and therefore more respectful towards the other person as well as more loving towards myself. I realise now that I don't have to spill my guts in the first five minutes to try and get a man to like me, but at that time I thought I was just being open and up front!

As a relationship addict, the 'hit' is as addictive as a cocaine high, or booze-fuelled binge, and as a depressed relationship addict I was almost grateful that my old despair had been replaced by a crush of momentous proportions! Think 'teenage obsession' and multiply it by 20.

However, the quality of my days began to be determined by whether I'd received email, and when I discovered that he was indeed married, I should have walked away. I seem to have a habit of picking men who don't want to, or cannot, tell me the truth about themselves before it's too late. But then, how truthful was I? Was I really interested in the man or was I seeing him as a commodity that would simply fix me? But doing the 'right' thing is so boring, isn't it? Life is to be lived and experienced. These are the kind of messages we all deal with on a daily basis. It's tough to be tame when you want to be wild and when the rest of the world is cheering you on with a resounding 'go for it!'

A fellow sufferer once revealed how she would spend whole mornings texting her forbidden love from the ladies toilet at work. 'Textual intercourse,' she called it. When he replied, she could relax. When he didn't reply, she'd consume vast quantities of chocolate and chain-smoke her way through the day. She got the sack.

Unsurprisingly, email man and I eventually met face to face. Cue violins and stormy weather. As I walked to the pub where we were to meet I could hear my inner voice nagging at me. 'Clare, why are you doing this to yourself?' it said. 'You are sad, you are tired, and you are so vulnerable. Walk away! Walk away!' I ignored it and kept walking. When I arrived at the pub I tried to appear cool and in control, but underneath I was already starring in my own Hollywood remake of *Pride and Prejudice*. I was hooked. I didn't even know this man, but in the space of an hour I was already having his children and buying a spaghetti strap designer dress for the 'they meet by the lake at his stately home' scene. He was artistic, clever and funny. But, like me, he was very confused, and he was also very much in denial over his compulsive need to pursue extra-marital affairs. He was also, like me, a Christian. Clearly, we would make the perfect dysfunctional couple.

Looking back, I think there was a genuine connection but I sincerely believed that, on the strength of that meeting and 25 emails, I was in love. Feelings of intensity and drama alternated with a great sense of despair and isolation. Turning my back on such an intrigue was almost impossible. In fact, I am not sure that I did it in my own strength but I managed to end it, I believe, by the strength God somehow gave me before it really even began. I was hardly an innocent bystander in the business but I really believed the worst was now over. However, I had not anticipated the overwhelming feelings of loss. They were worse than any I had previously experienced. I checked my email twenty times a day, longed for his texts, longed for anything that would give me a high and prove to me that I was loved, because I was so incapable of loving myself and unable to believe that God had any regard for me. It drove me to near suicide.

In my more lucid moments, I could not understand how I could transfer my feelings of love from a man who I knew very well, my ex-boyfriend, to someone who I hardly knew at all. Projecting our feelings onto people we don't know is very common in love addiction. We pin all our hopes and fears on this one person, expect him to be our knight in shining armour – we've been fed on the fairy tales long enough – and then we blame the object of our so-called desire when he doesn't live up to our unrealistic expectations. In short, we make them our heroes, our rescuers, our saviours and our gods, and what human person can ever live up to that kind of expectation?

This was just another way of blocking the pain and avoiding the reality of grieving for a relationship that I had invested so much in, and the marriage before it. It was frightening how quickly it rendered me almost unable to function professionally and personally. I would vacuum with one hand, and that was on a good day, whilst reading a printed out email in the other. I lost weight and could not face seeing my friends. In short, I was abandoning myself as I had been, I felt, abandoned in that hospital in my childhood. This was painful and familiar behaviour.

Add to that the, as yet undiagnosed, depression and my own addictive nature, and the result was this overnight obsession that was totally overwhelming. Addictive disease, I believe, is progressive. It can never be removed, but only arrested. This was my rock bottom, the moment when I realised I couldn't go any lower. I felt, like Job, let down by God. I had no boils, sores or locusts to contend with, but the feelings that Job expressed in his pleadings with God were my feelings – psychological angst, deep inner pain and utter, utter hopelessness. On my knees I begged God to take away the obsessional thoughts, the pain and the anger. But nothing happened. I knew I needed help, but I did not know which blind alley to haul myself into. This was the dead end.

Psalm 103 was, for me, a profound source of comfort. It promises that God will heal us of all our diseases. It doesn't say that pain will go overnight. God's timing is very often different from our human deadlines. Faith for me is often a real struggle. I had paid lip-service to official Christianity for nearly twenty years, but I could not see why God would want me to experience such pain and isolation. I concentrated on what I hadn't got rather than what I had. Where were my perfect 2.4 children, my sports utility vehicle and my matching dinner plates? Where was the man who would look after me? What had I done wrong to deserve to be punished in such a way? Why did I value my life so little? It was as if I had an internal stick I used to beat myself with. I had an inkling that my idea of a punitive and angry God was probably flawed, but I did not know how to change my perspective.

If, of course, I was inadequate or bad, then it would follow that God and everyone else would turn their backs on me. That's the logic of the wounded child, terrified of rejection yet clinging on to each crumb of affection, even if those scraps come from an inappropriate source. All in the mistaken belief that there will never be enough love to satisfy. I was effectively abandoning myself repeatedly and expecting others to rescue me. I was on my knees on the kitchen floor, suicidal and hopeless. The cat wound her small body around mine as if trying to help. But I felt as though nothing could make a difference. How on earth was I going to get myself out of this pit? I needed proper, professional help.

SIX

Steps to Wholeness

$\mathcal{M}$y attempts at dealing with my eating disorder, as I have explained, had begun during my marriage. However, the addiction went deeper than the food – and it was that I needed to address. The Twelve Step fellowships have had the most profound effect on my recovery, and once I was willing to admit that I had reached a dead end or rock bottom, I decided to try them out.

Anything I say about the Twelve Step programme is my interpretation of it. The programme has traditions, or principles, that must be upheld to protect all those working within it. The eleventh tradition states that 'our public relations policy is based on attraction, rather than promotion'.[1] I am keen to adhere to this principle and I do not want to promote or publicise the Twelve Steps in any way that would hurt those within it. What I am writing here has not been endorsed by the Twelve Step fellowships.

However, my own journey has been so profoundly affected by the Twelve Step model and the people that I have met along the way that it would be difficult for me to write further without reference to it. The Twelve Step programme is not a religion or cult, although it has its share of fundamentalist followers. It is basically a set of tools to enable the recovering addict to live life to the full, and it helps to arrest the impact of addiction.

I had dabbled with this fellowship at the suggestion

of my therapist as I began my painful recovery from bulimia. I was never fully committed and went to meetings sporadically. Now I was divorced and in my late thirties and those 15 years of overeating and then purging seemed to be over. I had started to go to my first meetings towards the end of this time, and I had managed to eat less chaotically and stop the vomiting. What I hadn't learned was how to nourish myself emotionally and spiritually. Now I decided to show up at meetings more often and, as I was to discover, the spiritual part of the programme was key to helping me to gain some eventual serenity.

No matter how many churches I attended, sermons I heard, counsellors I spoke to, or self-help books I bought, or how much I tried to appear as the epitome of independent cool, I still believed, after my divorce, that if I could only find the right relationship then I would find my ultimate answer. The first step in the Twelve Step programme is the key to understanding addiction and beginning the life-long process of dealing with it. 'We admitted we were powerless over alcohol/food/ relationships/drugs, and our lives had become unmanageable.' Crouched in that foetal position on the kitchen floor, in withdrawal after the email fiasco described in the last chapter, it occurred to me that I had no control whatsoever over this obsession of mine. No matter how hard I tried to let go, my mind kept bringing me back to my make-believe Hollywood hero; in this case, a married man with an apparently well thought-out and deep faith. In reality, he appeared to have as many problems as I did, and he would certainly not, logically, never mind morally, be healthy or good for me; and I would not be good for him, or his marriage.

The shame of that admission was overwhelming. I had internalised so many punitive sermons on the subject of sex outside of marriage, never mind a potentially adulterous affair with someone who was from within the Christian community. I had already crossed that boundary with my ex-boyfriend, never mind this newer liaison. Was there anyone else out there who understood? I felt alone and scared. How I longed for a preacher to say, 'Did you know that I had an affair?' or, 'My wife and I nearly got divorced many times; for months we lived as strangers.' I appreciate that sermons are not always the place to deliver Oprah Winfrey-style confessions, but I have found it hugely reassuring every time I have heard someone speaking honestly about his or her own struggles in this area.

The Bible, as I read it, is full of flawed, vulnerable and dysfunctional individuals. David, an adulterer and possibly the greatest psalmist of them all, could be described as the Bible's first prominent sex and love addict. He was also, in effect, a peeping tom, spying on the object of his sexual obsession – Bathsheba, a married woman. He has illicit sex with her, and then orders her husband, Uriah, to the battle front, knowing that he won't return. Her pregnancy means that the lust-driven king is forced to tie the knot, even though it looks as if he would have been perfectly content with a one-night stand. Who needs *Footballers' Wives* when you've got such colourful biblical lives?

Affairs, of course, do not always end in a brutal killing but, despite their forbidden and erotic pull, they often have terrible and painful consequences. I am the first to admit that. But ignoring the problem either personally, or in a Christian or Church environment, does not make it go away.

Fortunately I was able to find a Twelve Step fellowship where like-minded people shared their struggles with love, sex and relationship addiction. The meetings were held in a tatty community centre in central London, and the people came from many different backgrounds. But I have never felt such an overwhelming sense of relief at meeting others who had been suffering in exactly the same way as I had for so many years. As I spoke of my hopelessness and my compulsion to continue to communicate with a man who was bad for me, and my inability to stop, I felt love and support from the group. After one meeting, an older woman came over and hugged me. 'It *will* pass,' she said, 'but you are powerless. That is a painful lesson.' Powerlessness is an intriguing concept. As I began to acknowledge my own lack of control over my addiction to this man, or the idea of him, the obsession began to ease slightly. As I accepted my unmanageability in this area of my life, it became slightly more manageable. I realised, too, that following my divorce, I had a tendency to be attracted to men who were unavailable to me emotionally, spiritually and physically. It was as if I wanted to keep intimacy at arm's length in case I was trapped by a more available relationship. I realised I had become trapped anyway.

The idea of not being the ultimate master of our own destiny sits uneasily in our western culture. It is seductive to buy into the belief that people, jobs and possessions will bring us the security we crave. Of course, healthy relationships, work patterns and homes make a real difference to most human lives, but ultimately, I believe, we have no control over what happens to us. We can make certain choices, and we have free will to put those choices in place, but there is so much we cannot plan for or insure against, no matter how many pension plans we possess, or how hard we work out at the gym. I love the theologian Henri Nouwen's take on powerlessness. He writes, 'It is through total and unmitigated powerlessness that God shows us divine mercy.'[2] It seems a complete paradox that by admitting our need for God at such a deep level, our lives can be transformed and we can begin to find the freedom we crave.

My own attempts at trying to be a good Christian were just that – attempts at living up to a perceived model of goodness and holiness in my own strength. These attempts did not save me from my addictions; they simply reinforced my shame and increased my guilt at falling short of what I perceived to be the Christian ideal.

Once I admitted that I was helpless in trying to control my behaviour, I had no choice but to take the next step and 'come to believe that a power greater than ourselves could restore us to sanity.' Twelve Step is a collective, not an individualistic, programme, hence the word 'us' and not 'me'. It is not about individual self-improvement; it is about being part of a community that supports, listens and does not judge. It is not a church, nor is a Christian faith in any way a prerequisite of belonging. In fact, many struggle deeply with the idea of a higher power at all. However, in acknowledging, at a fundamental level, a need for that higher power, there is a shift of emphasis.

Sometimes, though, the feelings of abandonment and despair that are unleashed once an addict stops using their drug – be it a person or a substance – are so overwhelming that extra support can really help. Medical and psychological rehabilitation is expensive and time-consuming. But as I lay helpless and suicidal on that kitchen floor, I sensed that I needed another perspective. I was not a millionaire; I was a part-time theology student and journalist juggling my finances each month. My family's generosity contributed in part to the cost of treatment, and the process of asking for help was, in itself, healing and restorative.

My family, as mentioned before, tends to bury emotions. I am sure this is a very common British trait and blame is inappropriate – it's just the way things are. I will always be indebted to my parents and to my sister for their support at a time of great need, and in an area that, for them, must have been frightening and unfamiliar.

It is not possible for everyone to take time out of their lives and to begin full-time treatment, but for some of us it is one way to come to grips with the terror that accompanies the journey of discovery that begins once we let go of those substances or people we have used to anaesthetise our feelings. I felt as if my feelings would kill me, they were so strong. Of course that is not true, but when they have been buried for many years they can be overwhelming and terrifying. Rehab initially conjured up images, for me, of self-obsessed rock stars and neurotic supermodels who seem to have addictions like others have designer handbags, talking for hours about their trips abroad and swapping cosmetic surgery tips. The truth, as I discovered, was very different.

SEVEN

Rehab

$\mathcal{I}$ woke up in a sweat. The reason: it was my first encounter with day care at an 'official' rehab centre in the middle of London. I had hardly slept. My mind kept turning over, thinking, 'How did I get here? What is wrong with me? Why do I feel as if I have nothing to live for?' As I travelled on the tube I kept furtively glancing at my fellow passengers. 'They look so normal,' I said to myself; 'all of them on their way to work, or taking their kids to school. Doing the things that normal people do. Why can't I be like them?' A woman smiled at me and I wanted to weep with gratitude. I then became over-whelmed by panic and despair. What if they couldn't help me? What if my problems were so bad that I was a hopeless case? I subsequently discovered that most addicts think that their problems are unique and un-solvable. I am not a psychologist, and there are plenty of people with far greater expertise than I who have writ-ten about addiction and co-dependency. As I walked into the airy gym-like room and sat down with five people I didn't know and didn't really want to know, I had no idea how life-transforming the place and the people would prove to be.

'My name's Clare and I am addict,' were the first words I said. And then I cried for Britain. Admitting that I had an addictive problem to a roomful of strangers proved to be gut-wrenchingly terrifying but, ultimately, it was very liberating. The group continued as if I had been there for many weeks. When I shared bits of my story, 'I can't seem to put my relationship down; I don't seem to be able to exist without being in a relationship; it is as if I will die,' I saw heads nodding and no criticism came. I cried some more. As the day wore on I began to see the similarities, not the differences. I was in rehab with former drug dealers, wealthy heroin addicts, teenage marijuana users and tough and wonderful alcoholics. When I introduced myself as a love and relationship addict, I felt great shame and sadness, worrying that my peers would think I was a hooker or a social outcast. As it turned out, I received love not judgement, and most of them were struggling with relationships too. My theory, and it is only a theory, is that underneath most substance addictions lies the need to find that perfect relationship which will be the answer to all loneliness, despair and compulsion. In wider society, the belief that life will be perfect once we find 'the one' is a view that many non-addicts hold. Many people are not prepared to admit to this part of their nature, but when they do, they are surprised at how many others feel the same way. I had often dreamt of being able to be really honest with others about my demons, and I had only been able to do that with a few select people, some who would call themselves Christians and others who would not. Here I began to fully understand what being part of an honest community really meant. It was a prayer answered.

Each day we were in group therapy or 'group' as they called it. Each session was an hour long and consisted of drama therapy, art work, listening to someone else's story or simply sharing our own experience of one of the Twelve Steps. I spent eight hours a day in rehab, five days a week, for four weeks. The honesty of my fellow recovering addicts and the kindness and sensitivity of the counsellors was something of a shock at first. It was hard to share my innermost feelings with strangers, but also a great relief. I challenged my fellow group members just as they challenged me.

The most painful part of the treatment was the realisation that I had been using relationships to avoid facing my own abyss and depression. In order to begin to get well I was going to have to let all romantic relationships go so that I could address my demons. During one drama session another group member played my ex-boyfriend, and I acted as myself. We played out the possibility of letting him go. 'It's over,' I said. 'But ... we love each other,' came my fellow actor's reply. 'It's over,' I repeated again,' this time in tears. 'But you are depressed, you don't know your own mind,' came the role-play reply. And we went backwards and forwards until, finally, he got up and left the room, saying, 'I've had enough. I will leave *you* if you can't see sense.' I ended up on the wooden floor, screaming in pain. Through this reconstruction I realised that this was not real love. It was an attachment that was based on the fear of being alone, a fear that was rooted in my childhood.

After any traumatic session we were encouraged to stay close to the group, and we would all troop out for a cigarette to try and dull the feelings! It was the email liaison with the married man that had taken me into treatment, and despite my fragile emotional state I had resumed my relationship with my ex again as I could not bear to face all this alone. That is the challenge of addiction. It is deep-rooted and it can take many years to emerge from. Twelve Step recovery talks of the addictive disease being 'arrested', not actually cured. To change the behaviour takes time, many meetings, a lot of support and great humility from the addict as he or she realises that God, or her higher power, can fill the emptiness that the substance or person can't. It is not simply a question of doing recovery 'right', or praying and trying harder. Addictive disease is complex; it may also be mixed in with depression and other kinds of mental illness. I have learned to forgive myself for the constant toing and froing in this relationship. I was not capable of anything else at the time. It was actually because of my great desperation and fear that I had reconnected with my ex. There was love in the mix, but I was also in total confusion about who I was and what I really needed. I had also not addressed the deep depression that underpinned all my addictive behaviour. My ex was thrilled about our reunion, but very confused by my decision to go and get treatment. From his perspective I must have looked very manipulative, picking him up when I needed him and dropping him when I didn't. He, of course, had his own issues. Addicts tend to attract other addicts, and he could have walked away at any time. But he chose to return. Of course, trying to have a relationship when I was in such a state was impossible and we separated yet again. It was utter chaos. I wept a river of tears, feeling guilty, evil, cruel and just plain useless.

I felt as though I was being ripped apart, and I blamed myself completely for causing him so much agony. Although the treatment centre was supportive and encouraging, they neither condemned nor condoned the behaviour. It was only by praying and talking to God in the darkness of that time that I managed to hold onto some kind of sanity.

Despite the work that I did in rehab, each day was still a trial. The only respite I got was sleep, and when I awoke the pain kicked in so severely that I could not breathe. Thomas Moore, the theologian, former Catholic monk and counsellor puts it like this:

> Whether you are looking for love, or trying to make it work, it can be the most difficult challenge

in life and at times may seem absolutely impossible. The impossibility slowly cracks you open, teaches you the limits of human understanding, and gives you a bridge from the human to the divine.[1]

My own will had me clinging onto the relationship, like a drowning man clings onto a buoy. Step three offered another perspective: 'we made a decision to turn our will and our lives over to the care of God as we understood him'.

I will not be analysing each and every step in this book, as I have yet to finish them all. However, the first four in particular have helped to change my outlook and actions so I can talk about those with some authority. There can be a tendency within Twelve Step fellowships to become rigid and judgemental about how to 'do' the steps and how to 'do' recovery, particularly in the early days, when any recovering addict is frightened and vulnerable. Everyone is encouraged to 'take what they want, and leave the rest'.

Treatment was demanding, exhausting and expensive. For those four weeks we talked with and listened to each other. I had never encountered such honesty, such stubbornness, such denial, such pride and such humility all in one place. People realised that unless they were honest with themselves and with others then they ran the risk of relapse that, although temporarily pleasurable, would take them back to the hell from which they were trying to escape. There were rows and flashes of deep anger. One fellow addict ran out during a session to stock up on booze, only to return and start all over again. I was no better. I occasionally emailed my married fantasy man, blaming and shaming him for what was happening to me. I learned that he had gone on holiday with his wife. 'How could you?' I raged, calling him every name under the sun, imagining the two of them lovingly walking side by side on the beach and looking longingly into each other's eyes. I could not bear the idea of him being happy whilst I was suffering inside a classroom during the sweltering August heat.

The treatment was not perfect – there was a perspective on depression that I was later to find very difficult – but it was a start, a chance to open up and share things with other humans that had been buried for years and then had festered. During one art therapy session – and I can see the comedy in this – we were asked to explore our idea of what a higher power would be like. 'Can I use the glitter?' I asked, like a five-year-old. 'And the glue and that foil and feathers, too?' My paper, my hands and hair were covered in black paint and silver stars. This was Blue Peter with attitude. All I could conjure up was a black hole representing distance, judgement, hardness and punishment. I wept as I realised that the idea of a loving God was anathema to me; the concept just did not make sense. I saw God as conditional; if I was 'good' then I would be loved, if I was 'bad' then I would be abandoned.

Bizarrely, during this time, I was still studying for my diploma in theology at King's College in London (and having a nervous breakdown at the same time). I was also continuing to look at the possibility of ordination, and was due to meet with two 'examining chaplains' – people to whom a would-be priest can be referred by one of the Church of England's diocesan Director of Ordinands (DDO). My DDO was a very kind and wise woman, who I had already met and spoken with. But there was no way I could follow through with the chaplains' encounter. I was in bits, very vulnerable and very frightened, so I cancelled the meeting. I had never really understood how God could work with my frailty or weakness. I had learned, over the years to hide the pain so well.

Ironically, I got the initial call about going to see the chaplains two months before I went into treatment, whilst I was nursing a gin and tonic on my garden step on a very warm summer's night. The phone went, and simultaneously my doorbell rang; cue one rather guilty-looking and attractive, 'I'm married but ... ' man with a bottle of red wine in his hand. It was like two worlds colliding, and the irony of the timing was not lost on me. One minute I was asking for information about the examining chaplains – 'So who are they again?' The next, I was pouring a drink and asking why this man could be married yet be on my doorstep, flattered by the attention. I thank God that that phone call gave me some clarity and strength, when I thought I had none, to walk away rather unsteadily from what would, I am sure, have been a painful, although temporarily pleasurable encounter.

The other aspect to the ordination process was the decision to find what is rather grandly called a 'spiritual director'. The man I began to see, a priest, who I still meet with, helped me to look at my life and faith in new and revolutionary ways. He did not moralise or castigate me – I already knew that adultery was wrong and I didn't need to be reminded – but he showed me such compassion and love, and explained how my pattern of getting involved in someone else's 'dis-ease' (e.g. the married man's) would be a repetition of old behaviour and would not heal my own pain. Together we explored what unmet needs were being expressed by the addictive behaviour that I struggled so hard to conquer. 'God longs to move towards us, every bit of us, even our shadow side,' he said, and we worked for weeks looking at the Psalms, and focusing on God's regard for me as a human being. Having little or no regard for myself, this was at times an extraordinarily painful journey, but little by little I began to catch glimpses of how I was valued.

Rehab

The rehab continued; I had enough money for four weeks. I reorganised my working schedule and even though I was freelance, my regular employers were very supportive of my need to take some time off. I was also trying to complete my theology postgraduate diploma at the same time, and had begun to write my dissertation. I was studying the book of Job in the Old Testament, but I only got as far as writing two thousand words of a ten thousand-word essay when I realised that I would not make the deadline and that I would have to defer my studies for a year.

Later, I discovered that depression colours everything, including our outlook and our ability to see our lives clearly and objectively. Of course, I told myself, I had so much to be thankful for. I had my physical health, I was not on the poverty line, and I had not been caught up in a tsunami or a hurricane. So what was the problem? I have noticed that we live in a society that tells us we are 'entitled' to wealth, health and happiness. And that if those things elude us, the implication has to be that we are at fault and we deserve to be punished. That punishing attitude can also be replicated in some Christian views. 'If you don't think what we think or do as we do, you deserve whatever you get, God will see to it,' goes the mantra. 'We create our own luck', 'we reap what we sow', if we work hard we will be 'rewarded'. There is an element of truth in all those phrases, but none of them allow for the possibility of failure, mistakes, and mental illness. I felt as if I was being broken down, unravelled and dismantled brick by brick. All the things that I had put such faith in – my marriage, my prestigious job, my good income, and the degree that would give me even more status – were slipping through my fingers. If I was not a wife, a girlfriend, a broadcaster or a consumer, then what was I?

In 'group' I took some small steps that helped me to

begin to see that I was more than the labels I had lived by for so long. For years I had used an internal stick to beat myself from within. My childlike desire to please, and uncertainty about whether I was good enough, had turned into a monstrous internal judge and cruel puritan, which seemed to have a voice of its own. It criticised, found fault, disapproved and blamed. It was like a loud, punitive radio in my head that could not be silenced. 'You are weak, a whore,' it screeched. 'What has happened to your career and your dreams? You cannot even be married successfully. You are a complete waste of space!' I had turned the critical aspects of my parenting as a child into a living presence from which I could never escape as an adult. The reflection I got back from my fellow addicts was almost unrecognisable from the picture I had of myself inside. They described me as loving, talented, generous and stubborn, yet determined. In small ways, all of us in the room were given glimpses of ourselves as we really were. We were human beings with gifts and faults. We also all had a tendency to cover our sense of inadequacy with bravado and false pride, terrified that if we revealed our true selves we would be shunned or abandoned.

A number of people supported me during this time, and although some of them didn't really understand what was going on they were just there for me, a listening ear on the phone. My parents, too, were obviously worried, but were very kind and accepting about the whole event. My close friends were fantastic, supporting me in person and on the phone when I was in despair. The phone is an essential 'tool' in Twelve Step fellowships, a way of sharing our ups and downs with others who know what we are going through. Most 'civilians' would probably do this anyway, but for those of us who have difficulty asking for help and have hidden behind a mask of supposed strength for many years, asking for help, or just a listening ear, can be very daunting. 'Phoning a friend' when I was in need was a lot harder than simply ringing to ask for an answer to a difficult quiz question, as the TV show suggests. It meant letting them into my vulnerability, my emotions and fears. In return, they would phone me back and I would listen to their concerns and worries. It was like re-learning how to do relationships properly.

I also decided at this time to reconnect properly with a church. After five or six years of very sporadic church-going, I followed through some advice from my Director of Ordinands, and tentatively explored joining what's currently known as an 'emerging' church. Called 'Moot', it met on Sunday evenings in an existing Anglican church in Westminster, central London. The emphasis was on reflection and relationship with each other and with God. On my first visit there the community was sitting around a long table sharing supper. When we came to pray I began to cry, and in muddled words I tried to express how let down and alienated from God I felt. I said in this room of complete strangers, 'God, I feel let down, so alone, and such a failure. Why is this happening? What are you doing?' No one tried to comfort me or offer me an explanation, but I felt a deep respect and an accepting love from those around me. I was allowed to 'be' with red eyes and a runny nose. No one did a double take when I explained that I was in rehab and that I was struggling. There was no attempt to preach at me or to make the pain go away. I was simply held, and asked if I wanted to be prayed for. And then we talked about the weather! There was no drama, or judgement, just calm human concern.

This was also the first time I had been in a church service without having a panic attack. Ironic, when you think that I was considering becoming a priest. I'd be the first one in history to pass out every five minutes in the pulpit. Above all, the people and the service itself were gentle. I felt as though I was being 'loved' back into the kingdom of God.

It was intriguing, in my group therapy, how often religion or Christianity emerged as a talking point. It was not always in a positive light. Many had, like me, internalised a vicious, unforgiving God, who was out to punish and to humiliate. Others were riddled with Catholic guilt, and the one Muslim in the group was ashamed that he had let Allah down because of his heroin addiction. I did not feel the need to defend what little faith I had, or to justify it. I have always felt that God is big enough to deal with my frustration and others' disenchantment. Within Twelve Step groups we are all encouraged to trust a higher power. Many, because of abuse or deep hurt, or fatherly relationships that were lacking, cannot begin to associate trust with a paternalistic God. However, I noticed that in this environment, when people handed over their will and admitted their powerlessness, there was a real change in their lives. This was challenging and very reassuring all at the same time.

It is, of course, easy to blame institutions or people when we feel that we have been let down. Amongst the negative experiences there had been, for me, some huge positives: the Manchester vicar in my student years, who listened to my fears and cried alongside me; the Dean of Westminster Abbey, who I regularly met with over one summer, and who explained the significance of the communion when I revealed that, 'I find it hard to really "get" the resurrection and why should it really make a difference to me now, even though intellectually I understand it and have been a Christian for many years?'; and the CYFA youth leaders who shared their time and experience with me as an insecure teenager. At the risk of this sounding like an Oscar acceptance speech, I am also hugely indebted to my close friends, in and out of the Twelve Step fellowships, who refused to judge but simply loved me along the way; my parents and sister, who have always tried to help whenever they could; and of course my ex-husband and ex-boyfriend who did their best to support me, even if they didn't really understand the innermost workings of my mind.

When you are desperate you look for quick fix solutions. I have, over the years, tried to find 'answers' and solutions to my depression and addictions in numerous unorthodox places. I have learned to meditate using 'God have mercy' as way of focusing. This certainly helped to calm me down, although I prefer the mantra I was given on a meditation course that was not linked to any kind of faith tradition. I have been on life-improvement weekends with New Age gurus, and attended workshops with an emphasis on receiving 'abundance' in both my personal and public life. I learnt much from these experiences and I realised how many of us are looking for something more meaningful than the material. None of these experiences shook my faith in any way; in fact, they reinforced it. There is a lot of personal development trash teaching out there. Some of it makes me laugh heartily now. I remember being unable to share the enthusiasm of a fellow roommate at a holistic weekend retreat away. She had just had a colonic irrigation session and was ecstatic with the results. 'I ate sweetcorn last night,' she said breathlessly, 'and it's come through already . . . this is a miracle!' Even if she had been constipated for many days I am afraid I couldn't quite share her delight, but the absurdity of the situation was not lost on me. The fact is that desperate people will take desperate measures, and there is plenty out there to keep us busy and to deplete our bank accounts.

The Twelve Step community, though, has helped me

and my addictions most of all. The emphasis is on the community rather than the 'self', although personal sharing is a key part of the experience. To me, God, the Son and the Spirit, are also a 'community' – the Christian path is not merely a personal journey focusing upon self-improvement. Our western culture is rampantly individualistic; personal health, wealth and happiness are the goals we pursue. Why? 'Because I'm worth it,' says the shampoo ad. Neither Twelve Step nor the Bible says that these desires are wrong in themselves, but both imply that 'we' are in the journey together. We walk alongside our fellow men and women in our suffering and joys, and we share in theirs too; we are not just on our own personal path.

I realise, too, how much I want things to be black or white, right or wrong. I want God's healing now, and I want a relationship with God or another human being to be perfect this minute. This is what I call my fast-food mentality: 'Cheeseburger now, please, with fries and a large shake; immediately.' I want instant gratification. I don't like feeling miserable, depressed, angry or in pain. I have been used to, literally, medicating myself with food; filling my face and gut to avoid feelings. I pushed what I thought were 'bad' feelings down with chocolate and chips, or whatever was available at the late-night garage. Then there were the relationships that I embarked upon to try and ease the loneliness and despair. Of course, the agony is then buried deeper, and that pain inside increases in volume.

In treatment I began to learn that sad or dark feelings are not 'bad' or 'wrong', but they are part of being human. I have to take responsibility for those feelings, though. If someone hurts me, attacks me verbally, or is cruel or undermining, I can tell them that their behaviour is inappropriate, I can be angry and then deal with my pain. If I allow myself to be bullied or abused then I am allowing them too much power or autonomy. This, of course, does not apply to childhood abuse, domestic violence, verbal abuse or rape; anything where the 'victim' is unable to withstand the onslaught because of their age or situation. It is a way of moving away, as an adult, from blame, resentment and victim-like thinking.

I remember one of my rehab colleagues getting furious with me for saying that I thought he wasn't committed to recovery. 'Your father is paying all this money, and you can't even be bothered to turn up for sessions or you are late!' He told me to, 'Stop being so superior; you are just jealous because I have cash and you don't, and that I am younger than you with more opportunities ahead of me.' Painful though his comments were, he was right. He was often late and absent but I also had a deep resentment that he wasn't paying for his treatment himself. His rich businessman father was footing the bill, yet I was borrowing and scrimping to afford the care, as well as relying on my parents' generosity. I was also angry that I was in 'group' with teenagers and twenty-somethings who all, I thought, had time on their side.

This instance revealed the chip I have always had on my shoulder towards those I consider to have been born with a silver spoon in their mouths. My fellow addict may not have been committed to getting well, but by holding on to my resentment I was justifying my behaviour too, and reinforcing the view that I was always destined to be 'poor, victimised, forty-something Clare, always struggling and striving and always being given the short straw; if only I was rich and young then life would be better'. That mantra could equally be translated into, 'if only I had the right job/man/church then life would be so much rosier'. Also, to others, I may appear to be the one with the silver spoon – and that is not a true picture either. Let he who is without sin cast the first stone. The more I judge others, I notice, the harder a judge I am on myself.

I began this chapter looking at step three: 'we made a decision to turn our will and our lives over to the care of God as we understood him'. This is, of course, easier said than done, and it has hidden depths. Having acknowledged in step two that a higher power could restore me to sanity, it was then up to me to respond with some kind of action. For, me, my will had so often been a coping strategy. I used food to numb loneliness and to avoid uncomfortable feelings altogether, and I had turned to relationships for the same reason. To sit with those feelings, and not reach for what I believed would relieve them, was so, so hard. There is a difference between asking for help in a healthy way, and grabbing onto a person because of a fear of deep abandonment. It is also sometimes very hard to tell the difference between what is healthy and what is not. Step three teaches us that God will 'take care' of our lives if we allow ourselves to be 'taken out' of the driving seat. This does not mean that we don't have choices, but that the choices that we do make are not adrenalin-fuelled compulsions that stop us from feeling, temporarily, altogether.

In the past I had often believed that I was trusting God. Half the time that was a delusion. I thought I knew, deep down, what I wanted in terms of jobs, salaries and relationships, and I was determined to get it one way or another. That is not to say that God's will is always at odds with our own, but that sometimes what is best for us is not what we would always choose. I remember kneeling on the carpet after one TV audition, willing God to give me the job. 'I'll do anything. Pray harder, give my salary away, be kinder,' I promised. I was trying to control God to give *me* what I thought I wanted. To say, 'May your will be done' when you are in the midst of darkness is often more than any human is capable of.

At those times I learned to ask for the willingness to trust, and leave it at that. I remember chain-smoking on my garden doorstep after treatment (it is a favourite place of mine for reflection) and wanting, more than anything, to email the married would-be lover just to see that 'he was OK'. Of course that was not the truth — I was denying the reality. I wanted to fix myself and make 'myself OK' by doing so. I gritted my teeth, felt the pain and asked God for help, or phoned a friend, and the compulsion passed, leaving me with a sense of relief. I was not always successful in this endeavour but, like a small child, I made small steps as I got greater clarity, and as the obsession began to fade.

Human wilfulness is a strange quality. It conjures up an image of an impossible child throwing tantrums in supermarkets and toys out of the pram when they don't get what they want, when they want. However, I believe it to be more complex than that. It is ultimately, for me, fear-based. To trust that a situation will work out for the best sounds like a kind of naive optimism, the idea that every cloud has a silver lining. That is not what I mean. To trust, and put the will aside, is more a case of letting go of the outcome. In other words, no matter how much we want something or someone, we have, at some point, to let go of our desire to get it in a rigid and controlling way. If we do not — at least this is true for me — we can become obsessed with the endgame and, because we are human and cannot always see the whole picture, what we want may not be what is best for us. Let me give you an example.

I went for a meeting with a film production company on one of my days off from rehab treatment. It turned out that the director of the company had recently become a Christian and was pitching ideas around to a number of TV executives. Whilst we were talking about what I could offer him and what he could offer me, the conversation moved onto my difficult situation at the time. After he listened to my woes and complaints, he told me that I reminded him of the injured animal in Robert Redford's *The Horse Whisperer*. If you have seen the film you will know that the horse is badly hurt and deeply traumatised in a road accident, and so is the rider. To enable them both to get well they have to go against their human self-preservation instinct and trust that the 'horse whisperer' will help to heal them. Robert Redford's character has a long history of healing animals with bad track records that have been damaged in some way, but only if they submit to his will rather than pursue their own path. Time and time again the horse refuses to trust and fights back with all the energy it can muster, but finally it gives in, and slowly heals emotionally and physically. Its spirit is broken, in part, but it is transformed from a frightened, neurotic heap of bones into a calm and beautiful creature regaining its dignity in the process.

'You remind me of that horse,' he said, 'trying so hard to hang onto your own strength to avoid submission at any cost.' I went home after that meeting and rented the film. Part of me, my pride mainly, wanted to dismiss the analogy as corny and sentimental. But I could not stop myself from weeping as I could see how the relationship between the horse and its new master mirrored my relationship with God. It was not as though I was a deliberately malevolent or vicious person, but that I had built up coping strategies, over many years, in order to get what I thought would be the answer to the emptiness inside. I was essentially frightened of the pain inside, and I was terrified that these deep, dark feelings would overwhelm me if I stood still and let go of the reins. So often when I stopped working or wasn't 'in love', I felt an overwhelming darkness, like a heavy velvet cloak, burying me so deep that I felt I was falling into an abyss and would not be able to climb back out.

If I was going to take step three on board whole-heartedly it would mean taking a cold, hard look at who I was without shaming myself in the process, and learning new ways of coping with the stresses and strains of everyday life. In a sense, I had already begun to do this when I was able to walk away from the bulimia and face some of the feelings that emerged once I wasn't shoving them down with food. I discovered how angry I was. Great waves of rage would overwhelm me when I thought back to my hospital experience as a child. Great sadness struck me deep inside when I realised how much I longed to be closer to my parents although I knew, as an adult, that they had done the best they could. Huge resentment gripped me when I thought of all the high-profile TV and radio jobs that I felt should have been mine, but instead they had gone to someone else who, in a rather grandiose way, I considered to be less worthy.

Although addiction had clearly played a huge part in my life so far, it was the diagnosis that I was suffering from clinical depression that really shook me and got to the bottom of all the turmoil and pain. The overwhelming obsessive thoughts that I experienced, for instance during the email exchange with the 'I'm married but . . .' man, occurred at the height of a depression I hadn't recognised, or received proper treatment for. I am in no way trying to side-step responsibility for my life, but looking back my behaviour somehow makes more sense if I recognise the depressive element to my life. When those close to me suggested that I might be ill mentally, I didn't want to listen; I felt that that meant I really was a complete failure. An addict, a bulimic and a depressive – now there's something to really celebrate!

EIGHT

The Moody Blues

*D*epression – what is it? Why do we get it? Why did I get it? Why do I still have it? Why does God allow it? You know, I still don't have the answers to any of these questions, and if I am honest it is a real test of my faith. When all optimism goes, when joy is lost, and when my mind tells me, 'You are 45, single, with no kids and not much else to show for your life,' it is often hard to fight back and I cave in, grip my knuckles and just pray as best I can. I have some partial understanding of the illness, but as to *why* depression descends like a cloying gas on some of us and not on others, is still very much a mystery to me.

I do know, however, that it has been entwined with and possibly at the root of all my addictive behaviour. I didn't realise that it went so deep, and that I have probably been a sufferer from a very young age. It is a grief that always lurks at the bottom of my gut, a sense of unease that laces each day, even when the day is a good one; a fear that can grip at the most inappropriate moments – in the supermarket, at the bus stop, at the hairdressers. It cuts me off from my fellow human beings so that they seem far, far away, and I am left breathing inside a bubble, separated off from the rest of the world by a Perspex screen.

Praying harder does not make it go away. Asking for

forgiveness on my knees does not prompt it to disappear. Promising to be better, nicer, kinder and more loving only makes it worse. In short, it is a puzzling illness from which there doesn't seem to be much escape.

If you wanted this book to be a simple, 'I beat my eating disorder, my love addiction and my depression and the Lord healed me,' I am afraid you will be disappointed and I would have been dishonest. It is the truth that sets me free, and the truth about depression is that it is dark, excessively painful and very isolating. When I am in it, I find it hard to see that it will ever lift. I have felt, and sometimes still feel, abandoned by God. So did Job. So did David in the Psalms. I am, therefore, in good company. I don't doubt that God heals instantly, except that that always seems to happen to other people. I certainly haven't experienced it, and part of me really resents God for that. I want to feel brighter and better than I do, even though generally my mood is improving. I don't want to have to see a psychiatrist or therapist and talk about my 'feelings' or take medication – but that is my situation now, and I am trying to come to terms with it.

Following my spell in rehab over the summer, I slowly began to get my life back together. Well, it seemed that way, superficially at least. Christmas loomed in all its glittery glory, complete with parties, little black dresses and sparkly tops. But I had no one to share it with. Although I did all I could to try and stop myself contacting my ex-boyfriend, as I didn't want to mess up his life anymore than I had already, I found myself unable to keep away from the phone, and I called him up. He was, as always, thrilled to hear from me, and we arranged a few dates around New Year.

I hadn't, of course, really given myself time to process what had happened in the summer, and I was still unaware of the severe clinical depression that was yet to be diagnosed. Almost as soon as we met up I began to get panic attacks – I had to get up and sit on the loo all night, and I couldn't sleep or work. This, I realised, was nothing to do with him, but more to do with what he represented. I realised how much I loved him, but I also felt resentful that I didn't seem, still, after all this work, time and money, to be able to live without him.

Deep inside my psyche, for some reason, was the belief that if you loved someone you had to do what they wanted in order to keep that love, or else they would take it away. This was learned, I am sure, as a child. I remember as a small girl thinking that if my mother was upset and I tried to be good then everything would be all right and she would not be cross or angry but love me even more. In other words, my idea of love and my fear of rage or anger were rooted in the belief that love was conditional on how I behaved and how I acted.

This is the beginning of what is now called 'co-dependency' – the idea that we are responsible for everyone else's emotions, lives and business, that what we do or say will ultimately control how someone else will act or what they will do, and that their regard for us is conditional on how we behave or perform.

I am not in any way criticising my mother for what I have experienced as an adult, but I am sure that she learned harmful people-pleasing skills from her parents, as much as I would have learned them from her. I also learned many positive things but, as any reputable psychologist will tell you, it is in our families that we first build up the model of how 'we' are seen and how 'we' should act; we then tend to play this out in wider society. Our own individual personalities also play a part. My addictive nature may have simply been wired that way from birth. As I have mentioned before, there is great debate over whether an addictive 'gene' exists.

As I am sure you have gathered when you look at your own life, the way we are is always a combination of our nature and the way we are nurtured.

This does not, however, mean that our lives inevitably play out in a particular way, and that we are destined to be either a success or a failure. I still believe, although I find it very hard sometimes, that God can break through into some of the more fragmented parts of our personality and make them whole. Through the Twelve Steps and with the help of true friends, Christian or not, I have experienced healing in all my key relationships; whether with my parents, my friends or boyfriends. I choose to see this as part of God's work.

The reality of becoming aware of my love for this man, who I had treated so badly, and who reorganised his life so dramatically to be with me, plus the under-lying clinical depression that had yet to be properly diagnosed – despite the time in rehab – was too much and I was not able to function at all. Fortunately, I had a very experienced therapist who was able to identify what was clearly a depressive episode and she referred me immediately to a psychiatrist at the Priory Hospital in London.

This referral took me back to an experience years before with a psychiatrist at an NHS hospital in Nottingham where I was living with my ex-husband. I had been referred by my GP who was concerned about my food problems. I remember a corporate green office, uncomfortable chairs, and a smell of cabbage that emerged as I sat down opposite this man who attempted to grapple with the intricacies of my bulimia. This was over 20 years ago now, when eating disorders and their diagnosis was still something of a mystery amongst the medical profession.

The session, from where I was sitting, achieved nothing. He told me what I already knew: 'You have a preoccupation with food. It will probably right itself. Come back and see me in three months' time.' I left that room feeling humiliated and confused, but very clear that I could not be helped by this particular approach.

Imagine, then, my fear as I made my way to the Priory Hospital for my first appointment. I had read about the location in the pages of *Heat* magazine, and although I was only going to this particular place because this was where my new psychiatrist practised on a particular day, not because of its supposed celebrity status and prices, I felt that I had descended to the level of the self-obsessed, cosmetically-enhanced blondes who developed addictions like the rest of us developed rashes, and who languished in private hospital rooms taking calls from their agents and stylists. 'Hi, yes Johnny, I am in rehab. It's great, yah, kinda like a health farm with sexier doctors.'

Like everything I have described so far, the reality was far from the fantasy, although I could have sworn I saw someone from a well-known boy band on the grass by the entrance having a fag. The psychiatrist was kind, clear and professional. I had felt sick walking into her simple and functional room, and I had started to cry almost as soon as I sat down. I knew it would be all right when she handed me a huge box of Kleenex.

As soon as I began to talk, I broke down. 'I can't sleep, I can't eat and I feel completely useless, as though my life has been a complete waste of space.' She explained that the symptoms of clinical depression were more or less universal and listed just some of them: waking early, constant weeping, overwhelming anxiety, 'catastrophising' events so that I always believed that the worst outcome would occur and, possibly the most shameful admission of all, suicidal thinking. This may sound strange, but being able to talk openly with a professional about the suicidal thoughts that I had experienced over the last six months, just before rehab and during the months that followed, was a huge, unmitigated release and relief. I had already attended my own funeral in my fantasy head – it was to be a colourful event with KC and the Sunshine Band on the stereo, plenty of alcohol and jolly anecdotes from my nearest and dearest.

She listened as I told her why I felt such a failure. In a torrent of jumbled words I explained how felt. 'I've let down my ex-husband, God and my parents, I've screwed up the life of a dear ex-boyfriend who tried to stand by me, I've ruined the life of his ex-partner, and I have failed to achieve success or status in my professional career. Plus, I have this terrible sadness. All I have got to show for my years on this planet is part-ownership of a small one-bedroom flat in West London. It's such a little life.' I peeled off tissue after tissue, and wept into my lap.

I had voiced some of these thoughts before – to my current therapist at the time – but it felt different expressing what I thought were such unacceptable feelings in front of a medical professional who had spent over 20 years working with addicts, manic depressives and for whom mental illness was no stranger. I was so happy, in a macabre kind of way, to hear her diagnosis.

In a calm and loving way she explained her thoughts. 'You clearly have a bad episode of clinical depression, and I think you may have been battling with it for many years. The good news is, we can help with the right medication and the right therapeutic support.' 'But what about the Twelve Step programme,' I squeaked in exasperation, 'and the rehab I went through? Was that all a waste of time, money and effort?'

She said that in her clinical experience, the Twelve Step fellowships helped profoundly. 'I do not know why they do medically, but they seem to make a real difference. But it's difficult to "do" the steps whilst you're badly depressed; I think they might just become another "task" that you would feel you weren't completing. Medication can really help, if you get the right levels.' She explained how my serotonin levels, the feel-good chemicals in my brain, were much depleted after years of stress and strain. When I asked whether I was 'wrong', as an addict, to take antidepressants because that is what I had been told in my treatment centre. She was very categorical that 'one size does not fit all'; in other words, each person is different, each person presents similar symptoms but is prompted by different pressures, and each person needs to be treated as an individual.

She encouraged me to continue with the therapist I was already working with, and prescribed me a course of antidepressants to begin straight away. She also talked brutally and clinically about the impact of suicide on those around me. She was not emotional or loaded in her comments, but she explained clearly and logically that my continued suicidal thinking was a real sign of depression. 'If you choose to take your life, your family and relatives will find it hard to recover.' There was no hysteria or, 'You can't possibly think that', but a simple acceptance of where I was at emotionally, and a desire to help me recover. She also emphasised how important it was to be 'gentle' with myself.

As I walked down the stairs from her consulting room and out into the front garden I called one of my closest friends at the same time as lighting a cigarette. I wept down the phone as I told her, in a great jumble, what had happened, 'I am so relieved! At last, there is a name to all this pain.'

Retrospectively, I began to see that the head doctor was right. I am sure that I have been suffering from depression, be it in a mild form, for most of my adult life.

If you think you may be a fellow sufferer, I thoroughly recommend a book, given to me by my psychiatrist. In his book *Depressive Illness: the Curse of the Strong*, Dr Tim Cantopher lists the symptoms of the illness. Amongst them are early morning waking, loss of confidence, drive, patience, feelings, and so on. He also identifies depression as 'anger turned against the self'.[1]

As he explains, there are relatively few ways to deal with anger. It can be let out, as a toddler does at inappropriate times, sublimated, or turned into vigorous action, like sport. Or we can behave assertively and use our anger at appropriate times in appropriate ways. If we haven't learned to process our feelings properly, and I certainly hadn't, then they get stored up. Eventually, like a pressure cooker, these emotions will have to emerge, be it via depression or some kind of emotional collapse or breakdown.

This is obviously not a definitive view of depressive illness, but it certainly tallies with my own life. I don't remember getting angry at home with my family, except once over my A levels, when I swore at everyone and rushed to my room in tears. Clearly I had not allowed myself to express feelings of rage for years. The only way I had dealt with my anger in the past was to throw it all up, bulimic style, down the loo. That was my way of dealing with what I thought were inappropriate emotions. I certainly didn't believe that God really 'allowed' anger, and I thought that those darker emotions that we all possess should be kept well under wraps. How could God love an angry, vengeful, jealous and grieving human? It seemed beyond comprehension.

Looking back, I think I had sanitised the Christian teaching on this subject, and much of it was sanitised by those who taught it, and who were clearly out of touch with their own emotions; or so unable to contain their anger that it spilled over from the pulpit in the guise of vitriol and resentment at the 'non-Christians' out there, or the 'world, that puts itself first and Jesus last'.

My first job after leaving university was with Footprints, a theatre company working out of St Nicholas' Church in Nottingham. We performed in many parts of the UK, and on our travels we stayed with some amazing and some awful people. We also visited churches of every kind, shade and hue. At one Brethren service, all the women in our group (there were three of us out of five) were asked to cover our heads; at another we experienced hellfire and brimstone preaching from a Welsh pulpit; and in a London church we overheard a man spitting venom because a woman in the congregation, he thought, wore too much make-up (I heard him call her, under his breath, a 'whore'). That, of course says more about him, and his own repressed sexual responses, than anything else! We also visited some great places, where people were kind, warm and deeply loving.

In some ways it was a rewarding experience, only because working closely with four other individuals, and often being on the road with them for long periods of time, made me realise how human we all are, Christian or otherwise. It also made me aware of how often people working in a so-called Christian context are sometimes encouraged to present an image of themselves that is really not authentic; so we all end up pretending to be what we're not because of some perceived biblical notion of 'goodness' and because we are frightened that those around us will reject the 'real' us in all its messiness. That kind of pressure leads to all kinds of addictive behaviour and thinking.

In my time acting in Footprints, I was actively bulimic and one of my colleagues was a very active homosexual. He kept that part of his life secret – I loved him to bits – and everyone else had their issues too. Still, I believe now that God loves us all, dysfunction included; and as the theologian Henri Nouwen often emphasised, it can be the most wounded who can be the greatest help, providing, of course, that they know what those wounds are and are prepared to face them.

I mentioned suicidal thinking earlier in the chapter, and I want to explore this a little further. According to the Samaritans, there are 160,000 suicide attempts in this country every year, 5,000 people actually kill themselves, and who knows how many think about it. There is so much pressure to be cheerful come what may, and upbeat no matter what your circumstances might be, that if you are depressed it's hard to hold your head up high. And if you are a Christian and depressed, I think it is even harder. It shouldn't be, but it often is.

No matter how hard I prayed, meditated, beseeched God to heal me, bargained or pleaded, the depression did not disappear. I choose to think now that perhaps God can use my illness to allow others to feel the same way without shame, and to seek help. Though, frankly I'd rather not be so noble about it, but be as happy-go-lucky as the next person. Except the next person is never happy-go-lucky. Part of my suicidal thinking came from the constant comparing of my inner self with what I perceived I saw on someone else's outside. 'Compare and despair,' is what they call it in some Twelve Step groups. The truth is, you never really know what is going on in another person's mind or heart. That is God's domain – although I do sometimes think, by implication, that can make God a scary, meddling, controlling, know-it-all. However, I am sure you get my point.

I understand that we are not necessarily 'entitled' to be illness-free in our lives. That is just the way our world works, and there is plenty of theology out there looking at why suffering occurs. But despite that, anyone who is sad or sick will ask, 'Why me God?' It is a normal human response. I suppose we could equally ask, 'Why *not* me?' but entitlement in our culture is strong. We all are led to believe that we can 'have it all'. On the flip side of that, I cannot see the point of presenting a Christianity that is all about 'sacrifice, misery and pain'. 'Take up our cross' is all well and good, but surely that doesn't mean we shouldn't be allowed some joy along the way? I, for one, don't want to communicate a gospel that is without joy, humour and playfulness; but neither do I want to say that being a Christian, for me, has meant less pain and an easier life, as that would be dishonest. I think my faith has given me a perspective on pain. It's not always helped me to understand the reason for it, but I hold onto the fact that I am part of a bigger community when I suffer. I don't suffer alone; although, again, it was when I was at my most suicidal that I felt completely the opposite – abandoned, in despair and totally alone. I wish I *could* say that I felt God was with me at the time but, again, I vowed to be honest in this book and tell you how it *really* was, rather than say what I think you may want to hear.

It may be a cliché, but Christ's 'Garden of Gethsemane' experience gives me some comfort. It is here that he questions his impending death and crucifixion. The narrative in St Matthew's gospel in the New Testament is the description I find most moving: 'My Father, if it is possible, let this cup pass from me; yet not what I want, but what you want.'[2] When Jesus finds the disciples sleeping, possibly at the moment he needs their support most, he laments, 'the spirit is indeed willing, but the flesh is weak.'[3]

I can remember, often alone in my flat, weeping, shouting and cursing and screaming at God, 'So where is Jesus now? Why doesn't he come and save me from this terrible pain?' I couldn't move for sadness and agony. At the time I couldn't comprehend that Jesus

must have experienced all those emotions, but now I see
it a little more clearly.

NINE

A Helping Hand

So what are we to do, when we feel despair? The answer to this is to ask for help, ask for help, and ask for help again. But this raises some dilemmas. According to the psychiatrist Dr Tim Cantopher (whose book I mentioned in the previous chapter), those of us who are most likely to get depressed are those who are least likely to ask for support. It is as though asking for help is a kind of weakness. The chances are that your average depressed person, if there is such a thing, is a coper, comes from a family that copes, and is often the one that everyone else relies upon for support. They will also tend to be a high achiever, and have a tendency just to keep going no matter how miserable they feel, because to slow down and stop would be an admission of failure. Latest figures show that 20 per cent of us will, at some point, seek help for depression. This figure does not give us any idea of the number of those who won't – I imagine that depression is far more common than perhaps any of us realise. That is a considerable amount of misery and despair.

My plea would be, for God's sake – literally – tell someone. A trusted, non-judgmental friend, a colleague who you know to be loving and supportive, and of course your partner if you are in a relationship. Having said that, it took me ten years to seek help for my bulimia. That shows how proud and fearful I was about letting others into my pain. I am not beating myself up for that, but I really do appreciate how hard it is to admit to not feeling OK. I am not talking about the Monday morning blues here; I mean a mood that never lifts, hardly shifts, and leaves you feeling hopeless most of the time.

As I have described, I have found huge support in my Twelve Step fellowships and, more recently, possibly because I have been ready to be more open, at Moot, the church I am now fully part of in central London. Many GPs these days can show understanding but I would really recommend trying to get a referral to a good psychiatrist rather than just taking antidepressants without much supervision. If you do choose to go on medication it is very important to get the right sort of chemicals in your system, as there are so many out there. If you are able to manage without pills, then fine. But I really feel that there is no shame in medication if it is properly monitored. It is not, in any way, the ultimate answer. All my medication has done is quieten a busy and frantically anxious mind that would not sleep or rest. I still cry and sometimes feel blue. The pills have not numbed me out so that I cannot feel, and I don't want them to.

The other element to all of this is prayer, but not necessarily prayer as you may have known it. I was deeply touched when the priest who leads Moot, the church I am now part of, asked if he and the church could pray for me. I am convinced that somehow this is working slowly, but of course, I don't really know how. My own prayer life is increasingly not at all what it was when I first discovered my Christian faith.

One of the most constructive elements to feeling desperate has, strangely, been the shooting star kind of prayers that I have aimed in God's direction – the 'please help me', 'please lead me to decent loving people' kind of requests. I believe, by the grace of God, I have been led to meet people who have some idea of what I have been through. The exploration of ordination, which began as I started my diploma at King's College in London, has led me to meet those who have really been able to support me at my most desperate. And I really mean that. I often say to those who have never set foot inside a church, or who have no desire to explore Christianity at all, that Christians, for me, have been the worst and the best of people. I have met some who have shamed and blamed, and others who have loved and accepted. I have to say that the love and acceptance has often come from those who themselves have been vilified and criticised. I have a number of close friends from the Christian community who have shown me such love and kindness that I can hardly do their support justice in words. Equally, amongst my recovering addict friends, who come from all aspects of life, I have more often than not experienced a regard that I believe to be truly God-given. I am always intrigued at how those who may be at the very margins of the acceptable face of Christianity, and whose orientation and lifestyles so many may criticise, are often the least angry and the most loving. It's an observation that humbles me greatly.

My own prayer life has been non-existent, sporadic, sometimes focused, shopping-list orientated, bizarre, and nowadays less of a strain and more of an essential building block in my day. What I mean by prayer, though, is very different now from what it meant to me in the past.

I have essentially had to unlearn almost everything I ever learned about praying as a new convert. In those impressionable teenage days I prayed out loud with others, hoping that my prayers would 'fit in' with theirs. I prayed on my own, giving God a shopping list of wants as though he were a supermarket boss, and I awaited delivery of those desires with full-on enthusiasm. Post-divorce, seven years ago, I kept up a sort of dialogue, feeling unworthy of divine attention or notice. And thanks to King's College in London, my spiritual director, my current church and a chance encounter with a wonderful priest, my prayer life seems to have taken a form that fits into my personality, rather than fights it.

Twelve Step fellowships emphasise the spiritual nature of the recovery programme, but because they don't talk in Christian jargon I have been able to look anew at the way that I communicate with God, and I have learned from other recovering addicts more about trusting and believing than I have ever learned anywhere else. My spiritual director works with me on a six-weekly basis. We examine God's regard for me, and he suggests passages from the Bible that I can read and turn over in my head, sometimes even imagining myself in amongst the action.

I don't always feel up to reading the Bible at all, though. My psychiatrist was very concerned by how many academic books I was reading in order to finish my theology dissertation, and prescribed *Hello* and *Grazia* magazines as an antidote to all the heavy literature I had got absorbed in! It is so important, if you have depression, to still the brain rather than overload it, sit quietly rather than become over-energised. I am drawn now to a more meditative approach in my prayer life, and the most liberating technique of all is possibly the least demanding and the simplest. The chance encounter with the 'wonderful priest' that I mentioned earlier came about as I was exploring a television programme idea based on the subject of possession. She has a great expertise in this area and in healing, and she works closely with Church of England bishops in the area of exorcism.

We met at a local coffee shop near my office and I was transfixed by her kindness and grace. We were supposed to be talking about a TV project, but we moved quickly on to my own struggle with prayer: 'I find prayer so hard, I want to do it right, but I feel I am doing it all wrong.' She suggested that I simply 'sit' for 20 minutes once a day, or twice if I could manage it, and still my mind. I also sometimes say, over and over, 'God have mercy' in my head – it calms me down and quietens my mind.

This sitting silently, not having to 'do' or 'prove' anything, has been amazingly liberating. I no longer try so hard to define God but I simply sit and am still. Thoughts rush in and out of my head, the phone rings, the cat purrs and tries to sit on my chest, but I keep myself still if I can manage it for 20 minutes. Recently, in-between some anxious moments, I have been feeling more gratitude for my life, my home and my relationships. I have also felt much less compulsive around the areas of work, men and money. All this – which I believe is the grace of God – is revealed through my friends, loved ones, my church and by a spiritual source that I cannot fathom. To fathom it would be to attempt to define God, and I've long given up trying to do that!

This transformation is fragile, though, just as addiction is powerful and depressive illness slow to heal. The longer I have on this earth, the more I realise that trying to become some walking form of human perfection – kind, loving, prayerful, good at listening, slow to anger, and so on – is nigh on impossible. Of course, those qualities are to be admired, but I often find them in people who feel that they are failing and who are, simply because of their frailty, deeply attractive because you *know* that they have been through the mill.

Just a word, too, about what to do if someone you love is depressed or an addict themselves, and who may be in denial. This is material for a book in itself, but I will simply share some of the things I have learned on my own journey. It is tempting to try and fix someone who is depressed or addicted. By that I mean hiding bottles if they are an alcoholic, or suggesting ways that they might 'pull themselves out of it' if they are depressed. The first example is what they call in therapy-speak 'enabling' behaviour. That is, behaviour that stops the addict ultimately taking responsibility for his or her own 'dis-ease', and reaching what they call 'rock bottom'. That can be a very painful sight to behold. Someone you love, for example, ends up on the streets because they can no longer pay the rent due to spending their cash on booze. A child steals from your purse to buy drugs, because you won't hand over cash any more. There are hundreds of examples I could give here, all of them painful and difficult.

The key is to detach which is, as any parent or partner will know, sometimes almost impossible to do. This does not mean you don't love or care. In fact it was pointed out to me by a guest on my radio show that Jesus 'detached' about 40 times from those he had cared for or helped. He loved, and then let go. I have struggled with trying to 'control' people for most of my life, and I have come to the painful conclusion that it is impossible to change anyone but ourselves. Addicts are in denial until it gets too painful not to be. As long as you and I enable them to stay in the addiction that pain will be eased, and they may not seek help as quickly as they might if they are allowed to take their own path. This is so difficult to put into practice with children or teenagers, though; and I can understand a parent's dismay and determination to get their offspring off drugs or smoking whatever the cost. But ultimately if a child wants to 'use', they will.

As far as depression goes, I think it is important simply to 'be there' for someone who is ill. This is also an illness that won't disappear overnight; it is unlikely that the sufferer will snap out of it in a week or two.

Allowing a friend or loved one to weep, wail, or gnash their teeth in your company is in itself very healing. I have cried and sobbed at many a Twelve Step meeting, and because the rules state that no one can proffer advice or interrupt me whilst I'm doing it, I end up being surrounded by a handful of loving individuals who are simply listening to my pain. The healing impact of that is difficult to explain. Suffice it to say that there is something deeply loving about being allowed to cry in an accepting environment. I felt the same way when I first walked into Moot, my church, a couple of years ago. I was deeply depressed and when we prayed as a community I just began to weep quietly. I was grateful that no one rushed over to comfort me but just let me be. After the prayer session, people came over to acknowledge my feelings; there was no attempt to fix them. I will forever be grateful for that kind of love.

It is important too, with depression and addiction, to get professional help as soon as you feel able. If the denial is strong, then an addict will resist help at all cost. With depression, the sufferer may simply believe that they are a bit low, but they should be encouraged to at least see a GP if at all possible. Simply acknowledging feelings in this way can take a huge weight off the shoulders of the sufferer and their friends and family.

This is by no means a definitive list of what to do in these kinds of circumstances, and it took me many, many years to seek help at all. One of the difficult truths about addiction or depression is that we are ready to seek help when we are ready, and not before. I try never to tell people what they should or shouldn't do, even though it may be obvious to me that they would be better off out of a relationship, stopping drinking or taking coke or getting help with an eating disorder. I only make suggestions that they are free to follow or ignore. It is *their* journey, and I respect that. I pray, too, what I call a treacle prayer. I know it sounds bizarre, but I imagine God's love like treacle, surrounding those I love or who are in pain, soothing their ills and mopping their brows. And I ask God to give them what they need, not what I think they want or should have. Easy to do when you are praying for others, but when it comes to my own life, and trusting God for that, well that is a whole new challenge.

The last thing I want, and I believe other addicts or depressives want, are people feeling sorry for them. I am quite capable of feeling sorry for myself as well as being able to make decisions and mistakes, produce good work, and be a loyal friend and partner. However, I am aware that I have a tendency to be a 'half empty' person as opposed to a 'half full' one, and I have to be mindful that this can sometimes colour my judgement and perspective. It is also easy to hide behind illness of any kind. I am so used to feeling sad that to feel happy is unfamiliar. I know that, like many human beings, I tend to stick with what I know. It's as if pain is an ally and without it life would be rather flat and grey. The next stage on from that is the 'poor me' syndrome where I can wallow in misery and despair like mud. However, it not always easy to tell the difference between what is genuine depressive melancholy and self-indulgent negative thinking.

Fortunately, I have some very close friends who also suffer from depression in the same way. Strange though it may seem, we often laugh at ourselves and at other people's responses to the illness. One dear friend related the tale of her trip to the psychiatric nurse that she goes to see regularly. The nurse suggested that she put a Post-it note on her pillow on which she could write an affirming and comforting phrase; something like 'I love myself'. She was to say this to herself several times a day. Frankly, when you are the depths of a depressive episode, no quantity of positive Post-it notes would have an impact. We laughed about this and in doing so deepened our friendship.

That is generally what I find when I reveal my vulnerability. Obviously there is a time and place for showing others our innermost feelings and thoughts, and I have to be aware that there are many people who are deeply threatened by the idea that I may not be OK and that 'God didn't fix it overnight'. That, I believe, is their problem. But those who *can* see that life is complex and often difficult, be they believers or otherwise, I think breathe a sigh of relief when those of us who say we have a Christian faith are also prepared to admit our difficulties and struggles. Our faith, too, makes more sense to those around us when it is seen in the context of the challenge of human experience. That said, I have often cried out to God, 'Just give me an easy life, will you? I've had more than my fair share of woes for the time being! A lottery win and a prestigious job would do me just fine, thanks.'

I have to say that, although the support I received in rehab was invaluable, there was a belief there that depression was a state of mind that could be dealt with by working the Twelve Steps and staying with the feelings, however dark they became. I am afraid I part ways with my counsellors on this. They held the view that antidepressants were mood-altering, and were therefore no different to other addictive substances such as cocaine and heroin.

Having taken advice from other professionals who think differently, I now think that this is a simplistic and harmful perspective. I have since become aware that there are other treatment centres who acknowledge that depression and addiction are separate illnesses, and that while they may feed each other, they do each require appropriate treatment. Antidepressants, the

Twelve Steps and talking therapy may all be helpful in that process. Although that treatment had some positives, I was also frustrated by what I considered to be their simplistic perspective, and it took some time to deal with the anger.

There are 'fundamentals' in faith and in the Twelve Step fellowship, but these do not have to be interpreted rigidly or literally. Please don't think I am in any way diluting Christ, the cross, the resurrection, and its significance. I am trying to show my belief that it is important to be flexible and let God do the fundamentals. In other words, I believe that God exists whether I or anyone else chooses to believe or not. If Christianity is true, I need not be defensive, but I can trust that God knows how to handle even the most difficult person or situation. In a way, though, seeing flaws in my rehab treatment, although making me furious at first, was actually quite reassuring and prompted me to realise that churches are not the only places where human beings get things wrong, or act in a judgemental way. It is part of the human condition to seek certainty when we feel uncertain – to want things to be black and white when all around us and inside us there appears to be a maelstrom of confusion.

Certainty though, without any flexibility or perspective, can mean a set of rigid rules that imprison and fence in those who try to adhere to them. Studying theology helped me to challenge some of the more rigid ways of thinking that I had signed up to without really understanding their true meaning. Another of my favourite authors is Jeremy Young, a parish priest turned family therapist. In his book *The Cost of Certainty* he writes:

> ... the emotional reality is that only if God's love, forgiveness and acceptance are regarded as the

foundation and pre-condition for our ability to repent and change, rather than as the consequence of our repentance, will the Christian religion be able to function as a truly liberating and trans-formative system of belief. If not, it will inevitably create restrictive forms of religious practice, and bind believers in the chains of anxiety and fear.[1]

I realise, too, how much I want things to be black or white, right or wrong. I want God's healing now, and I want a relationship with God or another human being to be perfect this minute – my fast-food mentality.

Again, Jeremy Young's book, *The Cost of Certainty*, helped me to look at things in a new way. He writes:

I have been seeking to show how the Christian religion, especially when it asserts a false certainty, may become the enemy of both genuine faith and the growth to psychological maturity of its ad-herents ... conditional, exclusionary and dualistic forms of Christian belief, including the Gospel of Conditional Love [which states that God only for-gives and accepts into heaven those who have repented and come to believe in Jesus Christ] give rise to repression, neurosis and projection ... often Christians who accept these versions of Christian teaching injure their own souls because, in order to believe them, they engage in psychological splitting.[2]

I do not think he is saying anything heretical, but he emphasises the fact that Christ's death is meant to bring about reconciliation between God and humans and between the different parts of an individual's person-ality. I took from this book an understanding that all parts of me could be dealt with and redeemed by God and that, just possibly, the Christian journey could be

about accepting all aspects of myself, rather than burying the bits I felt were unlovable and unlikeable.

TEN

Onwards and Upwards

$\mathcal{I}$ always find it easier to make suggestions to other people about how they could improve their lives than look at ways I could change or allow God to change my own. The situation has eased since I have had greater clarity and the depression is not colouring my view on life in the way it used to. Before I received proper help everything was overwhelming. Making a meal, relating to people, going to work or church, and just getting up in the morning were all like climbing mountains. Now I find that I can cope with receiving a large electricity bill without crying and getting overdramatic ('Oh no, I will be cast out into the street because I haven't budgeted enough for it this month') and I can deal with conflict at work without thinking, 'That's it, they're going to sack me!'

I would not want to give the impression that now I find life easy all the time; it's often quite the opposite. But when I compare my life now with the way it was eight years ago, just after my divorce, it does seem as though I am able to deal with things more effectively without spiralling into a pit of despair. When it comes to compulsive and addictive behaviour and thinking, I have developed some techniques to help myself cope.

When I say 'I' have developed techniques, I really mean that I have learned them from others in the Twelve Step fellowships, and followed their suggestions. I have, also, with God's help, deepened my prayer life and stopped rushing about and doing quite so much.

Compulsive or obsessive thinking is deeply painful. It's as if the mind is possessed by some kind of demon of desire. When I described my obsession with the married man I met on email, it was like living in a cage or prison; I simply couldn't get him out of my mind. It was the same, many years before, when I was bulimic. I felt chocolate and cakes calling me, like Alice in Wonderland: 'Clare, eat me, taste me, have some more, eat me all up,' and I would feel edgy and ill at ease until I had binged until bursting. At each stage of my recovery I have learned to manage this obsession; and I have also learned that it gets worse the more depressed I am.

So, when I heard the 'I'm married but . . . ' man on the radio a few months ago, and my mind turned to the idea of contacting him to say 'Well done', in the guise of friendship, I examined my motives closely. What did I *really* want? I felt lonely at the time, there was something in me that wanted a 'fix', and believed that his attention would make me feel better about myself. When I heard him broadcasting and sounding carefree and confident I felt angry and resentful: 'How dare he sound so normal. Doesn't he know how much pain he caused *me*?' I then said step one: 'I am powerless over XXXX and my life becomes unmanageable.' I shared this minor obsessive thought – and believe me it was minor compared to past experience – with my friends at a meeting, and it left me. I look upon this as a mini-prayer that can be used in any circumstance. 'I am powerless over drink/cigarettes/food/other people and my life becomes unmanageable.' If you have ever tried to control behaviour, or another person, and failed miserably, you will know how painful the feelings of shame, failure and self-recrimination can be.

This tactic, if you can call it that, seems to work for me, although it can be very hard graft. In the early days of my food recovery I said it every ten seconds. It is, for me, a way of recognising my powerlessness, and asking my higher power to take away the compulsion. This is not the definitive answer to dealing with obsession, be it in thoughts or actions, but it is a reminder of my vulnerability and my need for the intervention of God or my higher power.

Having had the depression diagnosed appropriately, it is much easier to work the steps. As my psychiatrist said, 'How can you work the steps with a broken leg; in fact, how can you look at anything clearly when you are broken inside?' Exactly. That is what depression is like, a broken leg in the head. If you are in the depths of despair you will do almost anything to relieve yourself of that kind of misery. I know so much of my obsession around my relationships was linked to that. I don't like being in pain, and if I had the choice I would avoid it altogether. If the pain is so severe that it colours everything I do, then of course I am going to seek ways to boost the pleasure bits of my brain to give me some respite. It's a bit like trying to run a marathon with that broken leg; you can limp your way round the course, but you're never going to experience the run in a healthy way. I am so used to being hard on myself that it is very difficult to learn new ways of self-love. The phrase 'self-love' itself sounds self-indulgent and I immediately think of sermons that I have heard on the subject of losing self in order to follow Christ. But, as I mentioned before, how can we lose ourselves if we don't really have any idea of what or who we are?

So how do we begin that process of self-discovery? Or is that just an indulgence of a materialistic, self-obsessed culture that is up its own backside? Like any thing else, self-regard can easily become obsession. Ironically, self-obsession, I believe, occurs because we don't have enough self-regard. Let me explain.

When Jesus says, in St Matthew's gospel, 22:39, 'You shall love your neighbour as yourself', it is hard to make sense of that if we have little or no real self-love. If I believe that I am 'enough' as I am, I won't need to compulsively shop, take drugs, or throw up. Equally, I won't need to pursue one relationship after another in order to boost my flagging self-image. If I am as 'whole' as I can be, I will be able to shop without compulsion, eat lovingly, enjoy feeling ordinary without stimulants, and be able to give and accept love in my relationships without trying to control the other person. If I were like this one hundred per cent of the time, of course, I would be nigh-on perfect. But I hope you see what I am getting at.

During my first years in therapy when I was focused on simply trying to learn to eat properly, I remember the therapist talking about something she called 'the narcissistic wound'. One definition of narcissism is morbid self-love. As you probably know, Narcissus was the Greek god who was condemned to fall in love with his own reflection in the lake. Theologian and counsellor John Bradshaw examines this more closely:

> We humans would never know who we were without a mirror to look at in the beginning. The original mirror is almost always the person who raises us, especially in the first three years of life. The mothering person needs to mirror, admire and take us seriously. Obviously this is a tall order. Parents who never had these needs met themselves are themselves needy.[1]

He goes on to say that that neediness will be expressed by the parent's attempts to have their needs met by the child, thus the child becomes an instrument of the parent's will. Once this happens, he believes that the child's true self becomes abandoned and a false self emerges.

In other words, the child tries to be what he or she thinks the parent wants them to be, and never really succeeds. The child is then left with a constant feeling, deep down, that their true self is somehow bad or not good enough; thus they are set up for life to try and 'make' themselves feel better about themselves by any method that most suits their personality. And if they have inherited those addictive genes or brain pathways, you can see how the addictive process may sometimes kick in.

Now I am not saying that I was brought up badly or that my parents did not do the best they could with both my sister and me; that would be too easy an explanation. But I certainly learned that if I entertained my family I got love and attention, but if I was angry, rude or awkward that was not acceptable. My parents did have difficulty dealing with complex emotions, but so did and so do many families. I do think that one generation passes on problems to the next unless those problems are resolved in some way. But we also have to be sensitive to those who were brought up with different values and in a different time.

Nowadays, we are generally encouraged to be more open with our feelings – my parents' generation were encouraged to 'get on with it' rather than examine their emotions. Both approaches have their pros and cons, but it is important, if we do have compulsions or difficulty with relationships, to look at our childhoods so that we can determine which elements of our parenting were supportive and which elements we still carry with us, and that are potentially damaging. Are we constantly super-critical of ourselves, for example? We may have learned that from a parent who was often openly hard on us, but rarely praised us. Are we terrified when someone gets angry with us? We have learned that behaviour from our family because we have never actually seen our parents resolve an argument; therefore, anger holds great power and mystery and is to be avoided at all costs. Were we shamed for crying? I think this is particularly applicable to men. I personally have never had a problem with shedding tears! Perhaps men have been told to be strong little boys and that to cry is pathetic and weak.

I have a great sense of humour, and I can be very generous and kind. Those characteristics have always been celebrated in my family; in fact I am sure that I inherited them from my parents who are both very kind and amusing people, able to laugh at themselves in a way not everyone can. My mother is much loved by her friends and relatives and has spent many an hour helping older people enjoy their lives more, via much of her voluntary work. My father is fair and gentle, never snobbish or stuck up. He calls a spade a spade, and finds it hard to enter into my more 'emotional' world, and sometimes that hurts. But he is never sarcastic or cruel. It is important to celebrate the positive as well as be aware of the negative. Parents are human, too, of course; it is easy to forget that sometimes.

The other 'mirror', of course, is the one we look into when we try and communicate with God. What kind of reflection do we get back? And how much do we project our own deep psychological desires and wants onto a being that is impossible to define? All human beings are capable of reflecting God to some extent because, and I do believe this, we are created in God's image, male and female. So, when a friend, a parent, a partner, or a sibling loves us unconditionally, I choose to believe that this is God at work. It is hard, of course, when we feel that those who are supposed to share our faith are hard and judgemental. I am afraid I have experienced that

115

amongst Christians and I very much wanted things to be different. But I have also experienced judgement from those who don't profess any particular faith, so clearly judgemental behaviour is just part of being human and I, too, am quite capable of it.

I am convinced that the kind of God that we believe in will determine, to some extent, how we view ourselves. I have had real difficulty believing that the Christian God is a compassionate and loving father. There is so much 'smiting' and 'fighting' in the Old Testament; it is difficult to even approach the New Testament without the preconception that God is vengeful, angry and wrathful. If that is the God that has been communicated to us in our church or Christian group, then our response might be one of understandable and abject terror – a constant fear that if we step out of line, we will be struck down. We are back to the conditionality I mentioned in an earlier chapter, where we do a sort of 'deal' with God which really ends up being a 'deal' with the devil: if we are good enough, clever enough, loving enough, beautiful or thin enough, *then* we will be loved by God. What an impossible mountain to climb, and how much, with that kind of God in our heads, we set ourselves up for failure, self-loathing and disappointment! So what is the best way to heal and become more whole?

ELEVEN

Self Care

$\mathcal{I}$f I am to love others as I love myself then I need to learn to nourish and care for myself properly. This may sound completely bizarre in our western culture, where the message is 'put yourself first' and 'only the fittest survive'. But allow me to follow through. It is only in the last five years that I have learned to eat properly, only in the last two years that I have begun to learn to love adequately, and I am only learning now how to avoid spending compulsively. This feel-good society encourages us to 'treat ourselves' at every opportunity. This is a perfect mantra if we constantly feel that we are literally or metaphorically starving. If we have no idea how to use our spare time because we are always working to fill the void, or what to eat when we are alone because we are terrified of bingeing and putting on weight, then we are not going to know how to care for ourselves properly, and we are likely to grab any quick fix that will make us feel better about ourselves instantly.

Every time I see a new diet advertised I feel like screaming. 'Perfect thighs, in thirty days!' promises the advert. 'Do you want to be a size 00 like Posh?' 'The celebrity slimming fast that'll take inches off your jeans size!' And so on. If dieting were the answer then we would all be at our natural weight and at ease with our bodies. I do not know any woman who is entirely happy with the body she has. Dieting is so much about denial

117

and self-flagellation. Overeating or undereating is, I believe, about unacknowledged emotions. Get to grips with those, and we are less likely to starve ourselves or stuff our faces to numb the pain.

I recently made some soup for the first time. I know, let's hear a fanfare! Cooking has never been a great joy for me, even though my mother is a great hand at producing casseroles out of chicken carcases. Don't get too excited, I am hardly Delia Smith, but I no longer feel satisfied with constant junk or ready-made food (although a quarter-pounder can sometimes still hit the spot). I have discovered that I like listening to the radio whilst stirring or frying. I don't always have time, but when I do I really enjoy it. This is a brand new experience for me. Not so much the cooking but the discovery that I can enjoy it. After years of being terrified of food in all its incarnations, I no longer look at bread and think 'big bottom' or potatoes and think 'plump belly'. I may, shock horror, have even put on weight.

I have also wanted instant answers from God, too. I have longed for an overnight healing for my bulimia, a miraculous cure for my depression and an immediate solution to problems in my relationships. But I have had to wait, and, although this is incredibly hard to admit, I am almost glad that I have. I don't want to struggle all the time – and my depression was becoming too much of a burden to bear – but I can see how some of the pain has made me more compassionate and less hard on myself and on others. I wouldn't have chosen some of these afflictions, but now I have experienced them, perhaps they can be put to good use. I am certainly stronger than I used to be and more resilient. Perhaps in the future that strength will become something beautiful to behold. Perhaps I am exactly where I am meant to be, at this moment and at this time.

Interestingly, the more regard I have for myself in a

healthy way, the less likely I am to tolerate dysfunctional behaviour from others. I can spot emotional blackmail as if it was a police siren. I stand my ground if I sense I am being manipulated or controlled. I am much more in touch with my anger, as I am not masking it by bingeing or starving, and I try and let it out in appropriate ways. I try to be honest if I feel someone has upset me, or crossed a boundary that has caused me pain. I am, in a way, becoming more human, not less. And through that transformation I allow others to be more human too. If I can own my own feelings, then surely it gives them the freedom to own theirs? Bit by bit the true self emerges, setting us both free. I sense that this may sound a bit smug. I want to emphasise that all this is a work in progress; at times I am dishonest, I lack the courage to be truthful, and I don't always speak up if I have been hurt. However, I feel I am making slow progress towards being more open and truthful about who I am; in short, the shame is lifting.

To illustrate my point, I have just had to email someone I love because I feel that they have treated me indifferently. I wasn't full of rage or malicious in the message; I just explained how I felt, said that I hoped that they were ok, and that I still loved them, but I was unhappy with some aspects of their behaviour. In the old days I would have seethed and got more and more resentful. I would then have exploded, either at them or at something entirely unconnected with the situation, simply to get rid of the feelings. Going even further back in time, I would have bought a bagful of chocolate, stuffed my face with the lot and thrown it all up later. This is why it is good to honour all emotions, not just the ones we have learned were acceptable in our families, workplaces or churches.

I have talked about nourishing and nurturing the self a little, but I want to emphasise that I am still in the

119

process of working out what my hobbies are, not what to do to please other people. I feel ashamed that I am only discovering these things in my forties, but addictions arrest development, so in some ways it is a bit like having a delayed adolescence.

I am very aware that when I begin to obsess about anything, either external or internal (clothes, or my relationship with my close friends and family, for example), then there is always something else going on, a feeling that is being buried and not expressed properly. Then I have to sit with myself, or at least acknowledge that I don't know what's underneath the confusion, and trust God that he will reveal it to me.

Believe me when I say that I don't have time in the day for lots of navel-gazing or self-examination, but I have to be as aware of my feelings as I can be. Simply ignoring them means I will probably end up 'acting out' in inappropriate ways later, compulsively shopping or obsessing about work or a relationship, for example.

What so much of this boils down to is trust – trusting God and trusting ourselves. If we let go of trying to control the outcome then life will unfold naturally, in its own way. Every time I write down something like this I want to laugh at myself profoundly. Only last week I had flu and when I am ill the whole world feels as if it is falling down around me. I started to panic: 'I know I won't have enough money. I will starve. The cat will starve. I'll have my home repossessed.' A spot of 'catastrophising' as the psychiatrist would say. But sometimes I am gripped by so much fear that it takes my breath away.

This is the point at which I phone a friend in the Twelve Step fellowship, or I get myself to a meeting where I can share what is on my mind and heart. Meetings are, for me, like taking soothing medicine. They calm me down, and by listening to others feelings

I realise that I am not alone. There is great comfort in that. In sharing vulnerabilities we become stronger.

One of the most challenging things about this journey is that there is really no room for complacency. I don't mean that I am on edge all the time, but just that I have to be vigilant about the compulsions that come and go. If this makes me slightly self-obsessed or introspective, then so be it. I say it's what keeps me alive; recognising an obsession, acknowledging the true feeling around it – loneliness, frustration or anger, for example – sharing that feeling with another human and/or God, and then trying to let it go. That process helps me to stay 'clean', one day at a time at least. I don't believe that there is ever a 'cure' for addictive behaviour. Call it my thorn in the flesh if you like. I simply think it can be arrested on a daily basis. So how does the journey progress from here?

TWELVE

Continuing the Climb

$\mathcal{T}$here are Twelve Steps as you know, and I am about to do number seven. For me, each one takes much courage to complete. I have always liked to take my time with this kind of work, even though I also crave a quick solution. The steps are there as a gentle way to get well, not as another way we can shame and beat ourselves up. In step six ('We're entirely ready to have God remove all these defects of character') I listed all my defects or, as I like to call them, defences of character. These are ways that I have behaved in the past that meant I survived but they don't really serve me any more.

An example of this is the belief that I am a victim and that everyone and everything is out to get me. Certainly it felt that way when I got divorced but was that the true picture? Underneath, was it my guilt that motivated me to look this way at the world around me and at myself? It can be as much a defect or defence to value ourselves too little as it can be to value ourselves too much, for example by being pompous as a way of overcompensating for the fact that underneath we don't really believe we are loved or accepted.

Whenever I encounter pomposity or victim-like thinking, I always wonder what is going on underneath. What is the pompous teacher or TV presenter trying to hide? And for those who are always victims, what is the motivating fear behind the bitterness and anger of people for whom the world is always an angry, aggressive and evil place? Are they worried, deep down, that if things were sometimes good, and sometimes not so good – in other words, just ordinary – then they wouldn't have anything or anyone to blame, and they would have to look at their own behaviour instead? That's how I think sometimes. I don't like looking at my own part in things; I would rather blame someone else or something else out there.

A very moving story gripped me recently. A woman had left her marriage and her children to be on her own. She had been part of a Christian community and loved that part of her life but, 'They condemned me,' she said. 'All my so-called friends dropped me, or became threatened that I would steal their husbands. I am still a Christian and I see my children now at weekends, but the scapegoating and criticism and accusations were terrible. Everyone, including the priest said, "I must try harder". I had tried and I had to leave for my sanity.'

The story grabs my attention because it says a number of things. When people condemn I believe they do so because they are deeply threatened by another's behaviour. When someone breaks their rules, or challenges their world, there is a need to justify their position and make the other person 'wrong'; then the shaming and the shunning begins. The 'sinner' is ostracised by her peers, much like the woman at the well who had been married five times.[1] She had been ignored and outcast by her community. Why? Because they thought she was 'bad' and that her morality, or lack of it, was contaminating. Jesus spent time with her and gently identified her sickness; he did not condemn. 'Healthy people do not need a doctor,' he said, 'sick people do. I have not come to help "good" people. I came to tell sinners to repent.[2]' Sin is a loaded word. It is more often than not used to shame and diminish a human being. I believe Jesus meant that the woman's actions had separated her from God. God still loved her. In asking her to repent he was asking her to consider her position and think about whether it served her, as much as whether it was right or wrong.

I can't remember the number of times one of the faithful felt it 'their duty' to tell me that 'divorce was wrong'. I wanted to scream back. 'I know! I am punishing myself enough without you adding to the pressure! I find it hard enough to forgive myself, never mind believe that God forgives me.' Sin has separated me from God because I have bought into the belief that because I am divorced, I am therefore unworthy, tainted and diseased. But surely Jesus speaks to people like me? Surely God is concerned about people who know they are sick? Not those who feel they are 'good', or who are hiding their shame under a blanket of self-righteousness?

I have been in meetings and heard terrible stories of abuse and neglect. Yet an individual will still make their way through the step, grieving and raging when appropriate and taking responsibility when that's right too. It is important to be aware that many of us, myself included, who carry a lot of shame, have a tendency to take on too much responsibility for what has happened to us. In the case of one acquaintance of mine who was abused as a child, her tendency was to blame herself for what happened. She went over and over obsessively in her head all the occasions on which she and the abuser had met up and kept asking herself whether she had been provocative or had encouraged his behaviour. Yet she was only small and it was the adult who had abused her trust. It took her many months to get to grips with this. All I am saying is that we cannot do step six or seven or eight or nine until we have done the earlier groundwork.

The perfectionist in me would have liked to complete

all the steps before finishing this book but this hasn't been possible, I'm afraid. As the psychiatrist said, I must not push myself or do too much and I am already working full time as well as writing this. Over the last six months, for an hour every Saturday night I have written a little more, in small child-like steps. I have slowly moved towards the end tape. So it is with the steps and, to be truthful, we never really finish them. We continue to keep an inventory, as it is called, of our lives for as long as we live. Step seven is where I am at now, and it reads 'we humbly asked him/God/higher power, to remove our shortcomings.'

Having listed those shortcomings in step six, I now have to be ready for God to remove them. This is frightening. My shortcomings have been with me for a long time. Like my addictions, they are part friend and part foe; a familiar comfort blanket. If I am truly ready for God to intervene, what is going to be put in their place? Will I become this insipid, rather twee, individual who never has a bad word to say about anyone and is thoroughly boring and anodyne?

So, now I am nearly ready to do step seven and there's no going back. Based on past experience, each step has brought me a greater sense of self and greater happiness alongside considerable pain as I face myself as honestly as I can. There have been times when I haven't gone to meetings or actively followed the steps and my life has not fallen apart. Sometimes I have been, and sometimes I still am, angry at the process of recovery, for all the highs, the lows and the hard work I seem to have to put in just to stand still. But maybe I am not standing still. Maybe with each up and each down I am getting stronger and more aware – of God, of others, of the world around me and myself.

THIRTEEN

Can We Ever Fix It?

One of the most painful lessons I have had to learn throughout the last seven years of turmoil, treatment and recovery, is that nothing and no one is going to fix me, or fill the abyss. I would like to say that only God alone can do that. Well, in theory that should be true. But we don't live on the planet theory. If I am totally frank, I do still feel on occasions as though God *doesn't* hear me when I cry, but I just try and trust and act as though he does and keep up a dialogue, Job-style. Throughout the Bible, greater men and women than me have begged God to make himself known, and some-times they are left wanting. Does that make God a manipulative, whimsical tyrant? It certainly could look that way, but I think that is too easy an answer. In fact I don't think there is an answer.

The rather pally and matey God I talked to in my teens worked for me as a child. Now I am an adult, well, I doubt that God is less distant but he is more of a mystery; though, strangely on occasions, painfully immediate and for that I am grateful. Similarly, the Jesus I knew as a teenager – slightly trendy, rebellious and punk-like in my imagination – is now, well, what can I say, more weather-beaten, more bruised, more like me, I suppose. If I want a quick Christian fix, and believe me

I have asked for that many a time, I don't think I am going to get one.

Similarly, whether I am in a relationship or out of one, I still have to live with myself. I can often feel lonely when I am with other people, though that is easing, and I can be perfectly content simply being on my own provided I know that I have friends I love who I can call and talk to. It amazes me that I have spent virtually the last four days alone, writing this book. Twenty years ago, that would have been unheard of. Being alone for me used to bring up such terrible feelings of abandonment. My mind would have chattered endlessly, 'I can't go on. If I don't speak to someone soon I will cease to exist,' and so on. I remember at university being unable to stay in my room for one single minute; I found the feelings so overwhelming and terrifying.

When I am frightened, scared, hungry and or lonely, the tendency is to look to someone or something else to solve the crisis. A problem shared is a problem halved, certainly, but ultimately no one can live my life for me. I am already at least halfway through it, and I have really only just begun to realise that.

I also find freedom in the Trinity, in the mystery that means that God is three persons in one. For my theology diploma I had to write an essay about this, and it was daunting to say the least. But delving into past thinking about this subject was actually very liberating and demonstrates how study and knowledge can enlighten faith. Without overwhelming you with academic thinking, one much-loved theologian, the late Colin Gunton (who was a much-respected lecturer at King's College where I studied), highlights the relational aspect of this three-in-one scenario:

> Within the Trinity there is no hierarchy, God does not play separate roles, neither is he three separate

beings; a Trinitarian understanding of God is by definition a relational understanding.[1]

Now all of this quite meaty knowledge is not the stuff of everyday conversation on the bus. But it is intriguing how, for me, the studying I have done has trickled down into my psyche and added to my understanding and even, at times, helped to heal and ease the frustrations in my mind.

What I take away from all of this is the fact that God is, in essence, relational; within the Trinity there is no hierarchical pecking order. And, that engaging with God in the best way I can, by being honest and open, means that I, by some mystery, can become more fully human, more the person I was meant to be. Certainly, as this book has shown, I can lament, moan, complain, become angry with and hold resentments towards God, and have crises of faith. But I feel that God and I have journeyed a long way together, and I cannot really be bothered *not* to believe. It's as if the very act of being angry or honest about my emotions before this relational being, who clearly must understand the pain, allows me to connect with the buried bits of myself I have tried to hide from, with other people when I admit my vulnerability, and with God on those still rare occasions when I feel his presence. The fact that I sometimes doubt and despair does not disprove God at all. On the contrary, this allows me to believe in a God who is fully able to take on all my human suffering, for he made me this way! And the more honest I am about that suffering, the more real God becomes to me.

FOURTEEN

Work in Progress

$\mathcal{I}$ do believe that by a combination of working the steps and having been brought to my knees by my addictions in order to rebuild, I have begun to slowly improve my relationships with myself, those around me, and God. When I criticise others, for example, I examine what my part might be. I ask myself, 'What is it in my behaviour that needs to change? Do I need to be *more* loving of myself, not less? Do I need to be *more* honest about my anger with someone, rather than swallow it and allow it to breed like a cancer?' This goes back to the great dictum that I simply cannot change other people, and the harder I try to do that the more miserable and unhappy I become. I can only, with God's help, change myself. The irony of this is that when I change, sometimes those around me change too.

This principle can be applied at all times and in all circumstances. I am living in and trying to love in a society that is constantly seeking to blame others for the troubles we find ourselves in. Like a wounded child I stamp my feet and scream as toddlers do, pointing my finger at politicians, my friends, my bosses, and work colleagues, wailing, 'It's not fair! It's your fault. You're to blame. You're the reason why I am so unhappy, miserable unsuccessful, poor, angry, screwed up, addicted, unable to find a partner!' I know this, because I have said all of the above, and sometimes it needs to be said, in the privacy of my living room, or occasionally at a meeting where I need to let rip, knowing that I won't be interrupted. But when the rant is over, and I am exhausted and on my knees in defeat and frustration and there is no one else to blame or nowhere else to go, then I submit. It's like a dog when it's tired, when it rolls over and plays dead, or the spirited horse I mentioned earlier that struggled and fought and resisted before eventually trusting that its human trainers might want to help it rather than hinder it.

But it takes me a long time to get to this place and my pride won't let me go there often. Increasingly, though, this false pride does not serve me. It blocks the emotions that need to emerge, it compels me to present a false self to the rest of the world, and it undermines my relationship with God. Jane Austen's character Lizzie in *Pride and Prejudice* is right to home in on Mr Darcy's haughtiness and stuffiness. She can see that it is a front, but it is a front that stops him, and to some extent her, from being the people they want to be. When they rid themselves of it, they are able to communicate and connect in love. I've read the book about seven times and watched the latest film production on DVD about twelve times, so I know what I am talking about. Once an addictive personality, always an addictive personality, even if it's the telly that's the drug!

I am prideful when it comes to asking for help, and when I feel needy I despise myself for it. I have a great self-sufficiency gene that, for me, is really the enemy of intimacy with God and with other people. 'I can do this on my own,' goes my head, 'I don't need help, I don't need advice.' Letting people in on my vulnerability, petty jealousies, resentments and anger – all things that don't show me in a good light – is extremely difficult, but ultimately very liberating. I do not want my love relationships to be built on some fantasy or romantic notion that will fade as soon as the dustbins need to be emptied. I want them to be grounded in the earthiness of everyday life. That has to be a metaphor for my relationship with God as well. As much as God is a mystery he is still, I believe, interested in the ordinary. Take the lilies of the field passage:

> And why do you worry about clothing? Consider the lilies of the field, how they grow; they neither toil nor spin, yet I tell you, even Solomon in all his glory was not clothed like one of these. But if God so clothes the grass of the field, which is alive today and tomorrow is thrown in the oven, will he not much more clothe you – you of little faith![1]

I don't think this passage has anything to do with looking cool at London Fashion Week, or trying to be like Victoria Beckham and copy (if I had the money!) the accessories she's bought this month. I think, rather that it is about trust. I try to trust God for the small stuff as well as the grand life-changing events. It's a passage I worked on with my spiritual director. I simply imagined I was in a hot, sweet-smelling field, with a limited amount of cow dung around and optional designer sunglasses (!), having enough and being enough as I am.

One of the sad facts of life is that sometimes relationships don't work and no matter how hard I try to figure out why, once the anger and recrimination has subsided, I am left with the 'what ifs', 'if onlys' and 'I should haves'. A marriage ends, a partnership splits up, two best friends no longer see eye to eye; it's part of the cycle of life, this ending and moving on. I am sometimes asked which bit of the Bible I find the most compelling. I have always loved Ecclesiastes. I call it the Eeyore perspective. If you know *Winnie-the-Pooh* you will know that for Eeyore the glass is always half empty. The sky is falling in, everything is always going to end in disaster.

As he might say, 'whatisthepointofanythingasitallendsin miserysowemightaswellgiveupnow!' Ecclesiastes has a touch of that. Life is all ephemeral and transient, like the wind. Everything we put such effort into will pass eventually anyway. This is not actually a depressing book; I find it puts life into perspective. There is a 'time to mourn, a time to heal and a time to dance' as there is a time for everything. And there is also a time to let go. In fact, so much of my life so far has been about letting go. Letting go of old addictive habits and asking the emptiness to be filled on a daily basis, letting go of fantasy and replacing it with reality, letting go of an angry, punitive God and exploring the possibility of a loving relational power who may actually have my best interest at heart, and so on. In the letting go of old habits and behaviours there is much grief to go through; it is similar to the loss we experience when someone we love dies or we divorce. In many ways that grief is always a part of who we are, it just becomes a different shape and possibly less acute.

I always think of the death and the resurrection of Christ at this point. And I really am not trying to sound pious. In order for the new to emerge, the old has to die. In a love partnership or marriage there is always, I think, some loss of self as we become one with another human being. We do not become symbiotic with that other being as we are still separate and it is important to keep some of ourselves back, but there is a loss of sorts. When we move jobs we may lose contact with familiar colleagues as much as gain new experience in the next office or location. Seasons change as winter dies and spring emerges. I am sure you understand.

When Jesus talked about loss of self I like to think that maybe what he meant was that it is not about giving up everything we are or everything we like, sublimating our needs to accommodate everyone else and getting angry, but more about gaining a greater perspective via engagement and connection with others. In allowing people into my world, and in permitting them to see all of me – emotionally, I mean – then I somehow become more whole and more able to be me.

So when a relationship ends and we feel all that shame and guilt, as I still do from time to time about my divorce (I wish I didn't, but I do), there is the possibility that something new can emerge from that particular death and that hope and wholeness can be revisited.

I have just received the newsletter from my old school in Reading. It has the usual 'Births, Marriages and Deaths' section, plus news of old girls and current activities. There is also a form to fill in so you can update the Old Girls' Association about your life so far. As I read it in bed before I went to sleep last night, I laughed out loud at the thought of filling in that form. What do I put? 'Bulimic for 15 years, depressed for 6, divorced, been in rehab, no children, part-own a one-bedroom flat and have a cat!' Or do I write, 'Happy to be alive, wobble a lot from time to time but most days I have more peace of mind than I ever dreamt of!' Both lists are a far cry from what I think they want you to write: 'Successful career in the City, have four lovely children, own several acres with horses, have large, plush home with scented candles . . . ' That is an exaggeration, but you get my gist. I would like to be as honest in that newsletter as I am being here.

But I journey through today's heaven being vigilant. I try to let go of the things that stop me becoming the person God wants me to be and that stop me being whole and free, and I don't always succeed. By rights, I shouldn't really be alive; a 15-year eating disorder is a serious condition. But I am living, and increasingly it is no longer the half-life that I have experienced when I have been caught up in the terror and turmoil of all the compulsions I have described. I wouldn't have chosen to go through some of the pain but, by the grace of God, I have survived it just the same. I know I am not perfect and, thankfully, I am no longer in pursuit of some image of human perfection either in myself or in someone else. I have a greater self-regard these days, and the resulting self-obsession is subsiding. I am also part of a church that allows me to be honest, I have friends and loved ones who accept me for what I am, and a faith that may have been dealt some hearty blows, but that still sustains me. I still have questions, I still doubt, and I still wonder about the nature of this indefinable being who claims to love us unconditionally. But for today, I am enough. Aren't I?

The Serenity Prayer

God grant us the serenity to accept
the things we cannot change,
courage to change the things we can,
and the wisdom to know the difference.[2]

APPENDIX

Twelve Step Groups

Twelve Step meetings are held throughout the UK. Relevant groups include:

Alcoholics Anonymous
www.alcoholics-anonymous.org.uk

Sex and Love Addicts Anonymous
www.slaauk.org

Co-dependents Anonymous
www.coda-uk.org

Al-Anon
www.al-anonuk.org.uk

Sex Addicts Anonymous
www.sexaa.org

Overeaters Anonymous
www.oagb.org.uk

NOTES

Introduction
1. John Bradshaw, *Healing the Shame that Binds You* (Deerfield Beach, FL, Health Communications Inc., 1988), p. 67.
2. ibid., p. 15.

2. Family Matters
1. Henri J. M. Nouwen: *Life Signs: Intimacy, Fecundity and Ecstasy in Christian Perspective* (Garden City, NY, Doubleday, 1986), p. 67.

3. University Challenge
1. Pia Mellody, *Facing Love Addiction: Giving Yourself the Power to Change the Way You Love* (New York, HarperSanFrancisco, 1992), p. 3.

4. Career and Cravings
1. Briar Whitehead, *Craving for Love* (Tunbridge Wells, Monarch Books, 1993), p. 47.

6. Steps to Wholeness
1. Al-Anon Family Group, *Al-Anon's Twelve Steps and Twelve Traditions* (New York, Al-Anon Family Group Headquarters Inc., 1981), p. 131.
2. Henri J. M. Nouwen, *Finding My Way Home: Pathways to Life and the Spirit* (New York, Crossroad Publishing Company, 2001), p. 31.

7. Rehab
1. Thomas Moore, *Dark Nights of the Soul: a Guide to Finding*

Your Way through Life's Ordeals (London, Piatkus, 2004), p. 125.

8. The Moody Blues
1. Tim Cantopher, *Depressive Illness: the Curse of the Strong* (London, Sheldon Press, 2003), p. 17.
2. Matthew 26:39.
3. Matthew 26:41b.

9. A Helping Hand
1. Jeremy Young, *The Cost of Certainty* (London, Darton, Longman and Todd, 2004), p. 27.
2. ibid., pp. 150–51.

10. Onwards and Upwards
1. John Bradshaw, *Bradshaw on the Family* (Pompano Beach, FL, Health Communications, Florida, 1988), pp. 76–7.

12. Continuing the Climb
1. See John 4:4–26.
2. Luke 5:31–2.

13. Can We Ever Fix it?
1. Colin E. Gunton, *The Promise of Trinitarian Theology* (New York, T & T Clark, 2003), p. 110.

14. Work in Progress
1. Matthew 6:28–30.
2. Dr Rheinhold Niebuhr, theologian.

BIBLIOGRAPHY

Al-Anon Family Group, *Al-Anon's Twelve Steps and Twelve Traditions* (New York, Al-Anon Family Group Headquarters Inc., 1981).

John Bradshaw, *Bradshaw on the Family* (Pompano Beach, FL, Health Communications, 1988).

John Bradshaw, *Healing the Shame that Binds You* (Deerfield Beach, FL, Health Communications Inc., 1988).

Tim Cantopher, *Depressive Illness: the Curse of the Strong* (London, Sheldon Press, 2003).

Colin E. Gunton, *The Promise of Trinitarian Theology* (New York, T & T Clark, 2003).

Pia Mellody, *Facing Love Addiction: Giving Yourself the Power to Change the Way You Love* (New York, Harper-SanFrancisco, 1992).

Thomas Moore, *Dark Nights of the Soul: a Guide to Finding Your Way through Life's Ordeals* (London, Piatkus, 2004).

Henri J. M. Nouwen, *Finding My Way Home: Pathways to Life and the Spirit* (New York, Crossroad Publishing Company, 2001).

Henri J. M. Nouwen, *Life Signs: Intimacy, Fecundity and Ecstasy in Christian Perspective* (Garden City, NY, Doubleday, 1986).

Elaine Storkey, *The Search for Intimacy* (London, Hodder and Stoughton Ltd, 1995).

Briar Whitehead, *Craving for Love* (Tunbridge Wells, Monarch Books, 1993).

Jeremy Young, *The Cost of Certainty* (London, Darton, Longman and Todd, 2004).